Delma O. Lowery, Th.D.

Building Steadfast Christians

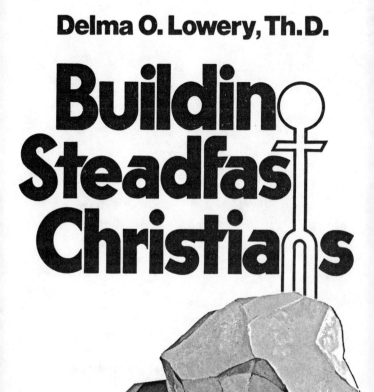

ISBN 0-9600920-1-3

Delma O. Lowery, Th.D.
Route 6, Box 336
Harriman, Tennessee 37748

Second Printing, 1980
Kingsport Press
Kingsport, Tennessee

ACKNOWLEDGMENTS

It would not be possible to acknowledge all who have contributed to my knowledge and understanding, thereby making the contents of this book possible. I should like to mention; however, the part my wife, Edna Lee, had in the production of this book by encouraging me and by spending many hours at the typewriter getting the manuscript ready for the publisher. Also, I should like to express my appreciation to the many pastors and laymen over the United States, and Canada, who read the manuscript and made suggestions or helpful comments.

Last of all, a special word of thanks is to be given to J. Mitchell Scott for the cover design and art work.

Sincerely,

Delma O. Lowery

FOREWORD

It is a joy to recommend the book, *Building Steadfast Christians,* by Dr. Delma Lowery. This is a thorough piece of work by a good pastor who worked dilgently to win souls and train new Christians to grow in grace.

Dr. Lowery is now in full-time Bible Conference work. His ministry has taken him to all parts of the nation and Canada. He has been acclaimed by pastors as a faithful preacher — teacher, a sound fundamentalist, and a fervent soul winner.

Here is a book for all Christians — new and old.

Sincerely,

Lee Roberson, Pastor
Highland Park Baptist Church
Chattanooga, Tennessee

TABLE OF CONTENTS

LIST OF CHARTS

PREFACE

In my past experience as a pastor, God has given a fair degree of success. One church more than doubled in attendance as a result of new converts being added to the church, and another church increased substantially as the result of an average of one new convert per week being added to the church. All new converts who submitted to baptism and affiliated with the church remained faithful in both cases. None were drop-outs. They all became steadfast christians. The reason for their stability and faithfulness is found in the fact that within one week after conversion, each one was given personal instructions, the contents of which are recorded in this book.

It is commonly said that seventy-five percent of all new converts who join a church cannot be found after three months. They do not become steadfast. If this statement is true, or if the truth is anywhere near the figures given in the statement, then there is a great need for an effective follow-up program which has been tried and proven.

While it is my opinion that all contained in this book is the least any new convert should be taught within a few weeks after conversion, it is my firm conviction that every new convert should be taught the contents of the first chapter within a week of his conversion. In fact,

I have found that the explanation of the contents of the first chapter is the best way to lead an unsaved person to a knowledge of Christ. The success has been overwhelming. Every lost person who has been willing to make an appointment with me for the purpose of having salvation explained to him has been saved. Such an explanation is time consuming, for it takes a minimum of two hours, but it is rewarding and yields lasting results.

While I lay no claim to perfection in my understanding and no claim to a flawless theology, I do feel certain that what is explained in this book is more comprehensive and understandable than what is explained to the greatest majority of converts, and that it will add a great deal to the understanding and assurance of many established christians.

This work goes forth; therefore, with the prayer that it will be widely used as a follow-up program for new converts, and as an establishing study course for other believers.

The Bible quotations are all from the King James Version, with the changes being my own as a result of my Greek studies. All changes are in parenthesis and are of two basic types. First, there are words inserted which do appear in the Greek text but are not translated into English in the King James Version. Secondly, there are words inserted which give a better translation of the word they follow.

CHAPTER I

WHAT ONE SHOULD KNOW ABOUT SALVATION

CHAPTER I

WHAT ONE SHOULD KNOW ABOUT SALVATION

Wherefore, as by one man sin entered into the world, and death by sin; and so death passed upon all men, for that all have sinned: (For until the law sin was in the world: but sin is not imputed when there is no law. Nevertheless death reigned from Adam to Moses, even over them that had not sinned after the similitude of Adam's transgression, who is the figure of him that was to come. But not as the offence, so also is the free gift. For if through the offence of one many be dead, much more the grace of God, and the gift by grace, which is by one man, Jesus Christ, hath abounded unto many. And not as it was by one that sinned, so is the gift: for the judgment was by one to condemnation, but the free gift is of many offences unto justification. For if by one man's offence death reigned by one; much more they which receive abundance of grace and of the gift of righteousness shall reign in life by one, Jesus Christ.) Therefore as by the offence of one judgment came upon all men to condemnation; even so by the righteousness of one the free gift came upon all men unto justification of life. For as by one man's disobedience many were made sinners, so by the obedience of one shall many be made righteous. Moreover the law entered, that the offence might abound. But where sin abounded, grace did much more abound: That as sin hath reigned unto death, even so might

*grace reign through righteousness unto eternal
life by Jesus Christ our Lord,* (*Romans 5:12-
21*).

This is the most important passage of
Scripture in all the Bible for understanding
what makes a person lost and what makes a
person saved, and what one is saved from and
what one is not saved from in Christ. Therefore,
a running expositional commentary of this
portion is very important.

THE INTRODUCTION OF DEATH

*Wherefore, as by one man sin entered into the
world, and death by sin; and so death passed
upon all men, for that all have sinned,* (*Romans
5:12*).

Very literally, the verse would read as
follows. "Wherefore, as through one man the
sin entered into the world (of humanity), and
the death through the sin; and so the death
passed unto all men, for that all sinned."

Notice that it was "through one man the sin
entered into the world." That one man, of
course, was Adam. Since, then, sin entered into
the world (of humanity) through Adam, it
logically follows that there was no sin in the
world of humanity before Adam sinned. There
was sin in the physical world before Adam
sinned because Satan was there to tempt Eve.

Notice also that death entered into the world
"through the sin." The "sin" through which
death entered the world was Adam's sin. It
should logically follow, then, that before Adam
sinned, there was no death in the world, and
that there would have been no death had he not
sinned. If he had not sinned, he could have lived

forever and populated the earth with a perfect people who would have lived forever, and the earth would not have become over populated during God's appointed time for mankind to inhabit the earth. We know this to be true because after God had placed Adam and Eve on the earth, He said to them, "Be fruitful, and multiply, and replenish (populate) the earth, and subdue it," (Genesis 1:28). After they had sinned, He said to the woman, "I will greatly multiply thy sorrow and thy conception," (Genesis 3:16). After death entered, conception had to be increased in order to multiply and populate the earth.

The next fact to note is that "the death passed unto all men." The death which came upon Adam was passed "unto all men." The last phrase of the verse states that "the death passed unto all men," why? "for that all sinned." This is not speaking of the fact that we have all sinned in this life which we are now living in the flesh, but of the life we had in Adam. It is true that we have all sinned, but that is not what brings death upon us. Many times, Romans 6:23 is quoted as a proof that our sinning is what causes death; "for the wages of sin is death." Notice that the word "sin" in the singular is used instead of sins or sinning. "Sin" in the singular speaks of "the sin" which was committed in Adam, while "sins" in the plural speaks of our personal actions in this life. In the book of Romans, almost every time that the word "sin" appears, the Greek text has the word "the" preceding it. This word designates a particular sin, "the sin" of Adam. So, "the wages of the sin is death." The sin "that all sinned" spoken of in Romans 5:12, which brought death to all men, then, is "the sin" which was committed in Adam. This does not mean that we must all die just because Adam sinned. Neither does it mean that the sin which he committed is imputed to us that we must suffer sin's consequence which is death. The statement "for that all sinned," means that all people sinned when Adam sinned.

One may ask the question, "How could I have sinned when Adam sinned when I wasn't there?" and the question would be legitimate. The answer is simple. You were there and you did sin the same sin which Adam sinned. We must remember that "the Lord God formed man of the dust of the ground, and breathed into his nostrils the breath of life; and man became a living soul," (Genesis 2:7). The Hebrew word which is rendered "life" is a plural word and should be rendered "lives." Therefore, God "breathed into his nostrils the breath of lives." Since the breath of all lives was breathed into Adam, then all people were present in him genetically. We must remember also that Eve was taken from Adam, and; therefore, had the same genetic characteristics as Adam to be passed on. "And Adam said, This is now bone of my bones, and flesh of my flesh: she shall be called woman, because she was taken out of man," (Genesis 2:23). Had Adam and Eve reproduced before they sinned, they would have passed on the same perfect genetic characteristics which they possessed, and the Spirit would have also been with the offsprings. Therefore, the offsprings would have been just like their parents, and having the same perfect environment would have acted and reacted the same way as Adam and Eve. Consequently, had any other man and / or woman been there in body as was Adam and Eve, they would have done exactly what Adam and Eve did. Hence, when Adam sinned, we all sinned. Today, we all have individual differences: first, because the genetic inheritance is no longer perfect because of the sin and fall of man, and; second, because our environments are all different since we all must deal with different people having different make-ups, while being different to everyone else ourselves. We see then that "death passed unto all men" because all sinned when Adam sinned. But what is death? Death is simply separation. The Bible speaks of three kinds of death or separations, and all three of them are in view in Romans 5:12.

THERE IS A SPIRITUAL DEATH

First, there is a spiritual death which is a state into which all people are born. The spiritual death took place the instant Adam sinned and has been the state of all mankind since that time. The spiritual death was not man's spirit "dying within him," whatever that would mean; but it was the separation of the Spirit of God from man. When the Spirit of God separated from man, he was immediately left to his own human spirit of life and conscience to direct him. These, of course, were susceptible to the influence of Satan and the desires of the flesh. Being apart from the Spirit of God, man was no longer perfect in any aspect of his being, and evil ruled. Since the only people existing at that time were Adam and Eve, and since they were fallen and had a sinful nature and flesh, all that they could reproduce was a fallen sinful nature and flesh, because like reproduces like. Job said, "Who can bring a clean thing from an unclean? not one," (Job 14:4). David said, "Behold, I was shapen in iniquity; and in sin did my mother conceive me," (Psalm 51:5). Jesus said, "That which is born of the flesh is flesh,"

(John 3:6). Therefore, all people by birth and nature are sinful and separated from God in the spiritual death. However, this state of spiritual death can be reversed to a state of spiritual life through the regeneration or renewing of the Holy Spirit.

But after that the kindness and love of God our Saviour toward man appeared, Not by works of righteousness which we have done, but according to his mercy he saved us, by the washing of regeneration, and renewing of the Holy Ghost; Which he shed on us abundantly through Jesus Christ our Saviour; That being justified by his grace, we should be made heirs according to the hope of eternal life, (Titus 3:4-7).

Many times we hear the phrase "the regeneration of the Holy Spirit" used by teachers, ministers, and laymen, and then they proceed to discuss the subject as if it were "regeneration by the Holy Spirit." There is a vast difference. "Regeneration by the Holy Spirit" would be something that the Holy Spirit does to the person, whereas "regeneration of the Holy Spirit," which is the Biblical usage of the phrase, would be something that happens to the Holy Spirit Himself. Notice that Titus 3:5, not only says "regeneration" of the Holy Spirit, but also says "renewing" of the Holy Spirit. We must consider the meaning of these words. "Re" means again, and "generate" means to produce; hence, to produce again. "Renew" means to re-establish or to cause to exist again. Basically, the meaning of these two terms is the same; to produce again or to cause to exist again. To rebuild a house or rewrite a paper means to produce them again or cause them to exist again. This is exactly what happens with the regeneration and renewing of the Holy Spirit. At the new birth or regeneration, it is not the new birth or regeneration of the person (you or me) but of the Holy Spirit Himself. At the regeneration or new birth, the Holy Spirit of God who was separated from man in the spiritual death is caused to exist in man again — the Holy Spirit is reborn, regenerated, or reproduced in man again. This is what Jesus meant when He said to Nicodemus, that a man must be "born again (from above)," (John 3:3). Nicodemus did not understand and asked, "How can a man be born when he is old? can he enter the second time into his mother's womb, and be born?" (John 3:4). Nicodemus was like many people today in that he thought of the new birth as the rebirth of the person. Jesus answered by saying, "That which is born of (out of) the flesh is flesh; and that which is born of (out of) the Spirit is Spirit," (John 3:6). That which is born from parents of human flesh is human flesh, but that which is born forth from God, Who is a Spirit, is Spirit. Peter said that we are "partakers of the Divine nature," (II Peter 1:4). How are we partakers of the Divine nature? By having the presence of the Holy Spirit of God in us who entered by regeneration. Paul said, "Christ in you," (Colossians 1:27). How is Christ in the believer? In the person of the Holy Spirit. We see then, that the spiritual death is the separation of the Spirit of God from man, and that the regeneration or new birth is the rebirth or reproduction of the Holy Spirit into man. This being true, many have asked the question, "If the regeneration or new birth is the re-entry of the perfect nature of God into man in the person of the Holy Spirit, why are saved people not perfect and why are the

19

children born to christian parents not perfect?"
The question is very logical, and also has a very
logical Scriptural answer. When the new birth
takes place and one is saved, it is only the soul
and spirit of man that is saved, not the body. We
are sealed by the Holy Spirit or given the
earnest of the Holy Spirit to assure or
guarantee us that He will one day save the body
at the resurrection.

*That we should be to the praise of his glory, who
first trusted in Christ. In whom ye also trusted,
after that ye heard the word of truth, the gospel
of your salvation: in whom also after that ye
believed, ye were sealed with that holy Spirit of
promise, Which is the earnest of our
inheritance until the redemption of the purchased possession, unto the praise of his glory,
(Ephesians 1:12-14).*

This question will be dealt with further under
the discussion of the physical death.
    Some people object to being spiritually dead
and lost because of the sin in Adam, and insist
that they should have the same opportunity and
choice which Adam had. People who think in
that manner should be reminded that they did
make a choice when Adam did, and that they
still have the same choice, except that it is in
reverse and easier. Adam was placed in this
physical life in a perfect state and given a
choice. He could either believe and obey God
and remain in a perfect state, or disbelieve and
disobey God and fall to an imperfect state and
condemnation. Adam deliberately chose the
latter. People who have entered the physical
life since Adam, have had the same choice in
reverse. They have entered this life in an imperfect state and condemned. They could either

disbelieve and reject God's offer and remain condemned, or they could believe and accept God's offer and be saved from the condemnation into a state of having the eternal Spirit of God within them Who would assure them of an eternal life of bliss. Many have deliberately made that latter choice which should be an easier decision than the one Adam had to make.

In summary, we see that the spiritual death is a spiritual separation, the separation of the Spirit of God from man; that the reversal of it is the new birth, renewing, or regenerating of the Holy Spirit into man; and that when the Holy Spirit enters a person through regeneration, He saves and seals the soul and spirit of man but only assures him of the future salvation of the body.

THERE IS AN ETERNAL SECOND DEATH

Secondly, there is a second death which is eternal. The second death is not second to physical death, but to the spiritual death. The first death, the spiritual death, is a state in which man is born but which can be reversed or annulled. The second death is a state and a place in which man remains for all eternity, for which there is no remedy once it has been entered into by one. "For the wages of (the) sin is death; but the (free) gift of God is eternal life through (in) Jesus Christ our Lord," (Romans 6:23). The death spoken of here is obviously eternal death, since it is contrasted with eternal life. The second death is a separation just as the first death is a separation. The first death is the separation of the Spirit of God from man, and the second death is the separation of the total man; body, soul, and spirit; from God into the eternal lake of fire for eternity.

And death and hell were cast into the lake of fire. This is the second death. And whosoever was not found written in the book of life was cast into the lake of fire, (Revelation 20:14-15).

But the fearful, and unbelieving, and the abominable, and murderers, and whoremongers, and sorcerers, and idolaters, and all liars, shall have their part in the lake which burneth with fire and brimstone: which is the second death, (Revelation 21:8).

Once this eternal death is entered into, it cannot be escaped; however, it may be avoided by redemption which is through the blood of Christ.

For there is one God, and one mediator between God and men, the man Christ Jesus; Who gave himself a ransom for all, to be testified in due time, (I Timothy 2:5-6).

Forasmuch as ye know that ye were not redeemed with corruptible things, as silver and gold, from your vain conversation received by tradition from your fathers; But with the precious blood of Christ, as of a lamb without blemish and without spot, (I Peter 1:18-19).

The word "ransom" refers to a price paid to buy something back, while the word "redeem" refers to the transaction of buying back. If one's child is kidnapped, the child is no longer in the possession of the parents but of another. The other person may demand a ransom price to be paid by the parents to buy the child back into their possession. This is the case with man and

God. Man belonged to God by virtue of creation, but through the sin in Adam was "sold under sin" and was destined for eternal destruction in the lake of fire. However, God was willing to pay the ransom price in order to buy man back unto Himself. This is the reason the death of Christ is called a ransom or a redemption. Having been purchased by the blood of Christ, we now have eternal life instead of eternal death upon or within us. In the book of the Revelation, we have a preview of a scene in heaven of those who will be redeemed from the earth by the blood of Christ. "And they sung a new song, saying, Thou art worthy to take the book, and to open the seals thereof: for thou wast slain, and hast redeemed us to God by thy blood out of every kindred, and tongue, and people, and nation," (Revelation 5:9). Since the redeemed have an eternal life which shall be lived in bliss with the Lord, then the opposite, eternal death, would be a life of eternal suffering separated from the Lord.

THERE IS A PHYSICAL DEATH

Thirdly, there is a physical death, which is the separation of the real person, soul and spirit, from the body. Concerning the believer, Paul said, "Therefore we are always confident, knowing that, whilst we are at home in the body, we are absent from the Lord," (II Corinthians 5:6). As long as the believer lives in his body, he is absent from the presence of the Lord, but as soon as he separates from his body, he goes to be present with the Lord. "We are confident, I say, and willing rather to be absent from the body, and to be present with the Lord," (II Corinthians 5:8). We see then that the physical death is simply the separation of the soul and spirit, the real person, from the body which returns to the dust from whence it came. "In the sweat of thy face shalt thou eat bread, till thou return unto the ground; for out of it wast thou taken: for dust thou art, and unto dust shalt thou return," (Genesis 3:19).

The physical death is not to be avoided, but will be overcome or undone by the resurrection. We are told by Paul that when Christ returns for His own, that those "which sleep in Jesus will God bring with Him," (I Thessalonians 4:14). In the same context, Paul states that "the dead in Christ shall rise first," (I Thessalonians 4:16). Notice that the souls and spirits of the redeemed are brought back from heaven with the Lord, and that the bodies of those redeemed ones are raised from the earth.

The reason the physical death has to take place with a believer, is because the body is not saved at the time of regeneration, only the soul and spirit. However, at the time the soul and spirit are saved and sealed by the Holy Spirit, the body is assured or guaranteed its salvation which takes place at the resurrection. Paul tells us that God has given us the earnest of the Holy Spirit to assure us of our resurrection.

Now he which stablisheth us with you in Christ, and hath anointed us, is God; Who hath also sealed us, and given the earnest of the Spirit in our hearts, (II Corinthians 1:21-22).

And grieve not the holy Spirit of God, whereby ye are sealed unto the day of redemption, (Ephesians 4:30).

Because of this truth, Paul states,

The creature (creation) itself also shall be delivered (freed) from the bondage of

24

corruption into the glorious liberty (freedom) of the children of God. For we know that the whole creation groaneth and travaileth in pain together until now. And not only they, but ourselves also, which have the firstfruits of the Spirit, even we ourselves groan within ourselves, waiting for the adoption, to wit, the redemption of our body, (Romans 8:21-23).

Therefore, the physical death which was brought upon man by the sin in Adam, is undone by the righteous act of Christ. "For since by man came death, by man came also the resurrection of the dead. For as in Adam all die, even so in Christ shall all be made alive. But every man in his own order: Christ the first-fruits; afterward they that are Christ's at his coming," (I Corinthians 15:21-23).

In summarizing, what we find in Romans 5:12 is that sin entered into the world of humanity through the man Adam, that death entered into the world through the sin in Adam, that the death which came unto Adam came unto all men because all men sinned when he sinned, and that death is three-fold. There is a spiritual death, which is the separation of the Spirit of God from man; there is an eternal second death, which is the eternal separation of the total person in body, soul, and spirit from God, into the eternal lake of fire; and there is a physical death, which is the separation of the soul and spirit from the present physical body. Thus, in verse twelve, we have the introduction of death.

We must now notice that verses thirteen through seventeen are in parenthesis, which indicate that these verses are given as further explanation of the subject introduced in verse twelve. In these verses, the Holy Spirit, through

Paul, gives a further explanation concerning the physical death, the eternal second death, and the spiritual death which we have just defined.

THE PHYSICAL DEATH

For until the law sin was in the world: but sin is not imputed when there is no law. Nevertheless (the) death reigned from Adam to (until) Moses, even over them. that had not sinned after the similitude of Adam's transgression, who is the figure (type) of (the) Him that was to come, (Romans 5:13-14).

In these two verses the physical death is spoken of, and no remedy is offered for it. The reason there is no remedy offered is because all people must pass through the gate of physical death to eternal bliss or to eternal separation and damnation. It is often stated that those living believers who are to be taken in the rapture will not die physically. We must remember, however, that the physical death is simply a separation of the soul and spirit from the present physical body. We must also remember that the Scriptures teach that "it is appointed unto men once to die, but after this the judgment," (Hebrews 9:27). Therefore, all men must die physically. When the rapture takes place, no christian will go up in his present physical body, but all living believers will be instantly separated from the mortal body of sin and enter into the perfect body which is like unto the glorious body of Christ. It is clear, then, that all believers will pass through the gate of physical death (separation), but not all believers will have to experience a time when their bodies are "sleeping" in death.

Behold, I shew you a mystery; We shall not all sleep, but we shall all be changed, In a moment, in the twinkling of an eye, at the last trump: for the trumpet shall sound, and the dead shall be raised incorruptible, and we shall be changed. For this corruptible must put on incorruption, and this mortal must put on immortality, (I Corinthians 15:51-53).

Now, notice that "sin was in the world" until the law. The word "sin" does not have the definite article preceding it, so it does not refer to the sin of Adam or the sin in Adam, but the presence and prevalence of sin in the world by all mankind. Notice also that this sin was in the world "until the law." From when until what law? one may ask. From the sin of Adam until the law which was given to Moses on Mount Sinai. We know that this is true because of the statement in verse fourteen which speaks of the same period of time by saying, "nevertheless death reigned from Adam to Moses." The next question we must ask is, "How long was it from the fall of Adam to the giving of the law?" In round figures, the answer would be, about two thousand and five hundred years. In other words, sin was in the world for the first twenty-five hundred years; "but sin is not imputed when there is no law." The word "imputed" simply means to count to one's charge or to charge to one's account. The English word "imputed" is found in the New Testament several times, but the word which is rendered as "imputed" in this passage is found only one other time in the New Testament; Philemon, eighteen. This word carries the meaning of placing on one's account that which is really his. The word "imputed" as found in reference to Abraham because he believed God, has a

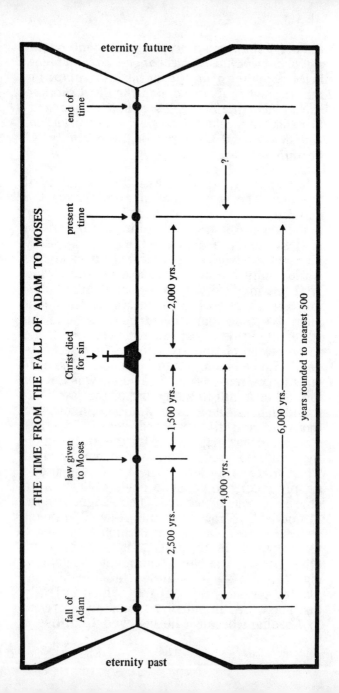

THE TIME FROM THE FALL OF ADAM TO MOSES

eternity future

eternity past

end of time

present time

Christ died for sin

law given to Moses

fall of Adam

?

2,000 yrs.

1,500 yrs.

2,500 yrs.

4,000 yrs.

6,000 yrs.

years rounded to nearest 500

different meaning. "And therefore it was imputed to him for righteousness," (Romans 4:22). The word "imputed" which is used here carries the meaning of reckoning or placing on one's account that which is not really his. This is what happens when the righteousness of Christ is "imputed" to us or placed on our account. Therefore, since sin is "not imputed" when there is no law, for the first twenty-five hundred years that man was upon the earth he did not have his personal actions of sin counted against him.

Let us suppose that before automobiles became popular in the United States, and before any traffic laws were established, that someone was able to "soup-up" the engine of his car so that it would run one hundred and fifty miles per hour. Now, let us suppose that he actually drove that car at one hundred and fifty miles per hour. He certainly could not have been charged with doing wrong because there were no speed or traffic laws. However, he was doing wrong morally, because he was endangering the life and property of other people. Just so, mankind was doing moral wrong in the sight of God for the first twenty-five hundred years, but did not have it counted against him because there was no law.

"Nevertheless death reigned from Adam to Moses." That is, physical death held authority over all mankind from Adam to Moses, and all; therefore, had to die. The question which we may raise at this point is simply this: If, according to verse twelve, the reason people die is because of sin; and if, according to verse thirteen, the people who lived on the earth for the first twenty-five hundred years had no personal actions of sins counted against them; and if, according to verse fourteen, they all had to die anyway, for what reason did they die? For the answer to this question, we must remember that the sin of Adam was not a sin imputed to mankind which was not theirs, but a sin which all men committed in Adam. Therefore, we see that physical death is upon mankind because of the sin in Adam, and not because of personal actions of sin in this life, because the people who lived before the law and had no personal sins counted to their charge also had to die.

When we understand this, the remainder of verse fourteen is relatively simple, for we see that death reigned or had authority from Adam to Moses, "even over them that had not sinned after the similitude of Adam's transgression." Adam transgressed or sinned against God by deliberately disobeying a direct command from God. The greatest majority of the people who lived between the time of Adam and the time of Moses did not receive a direct command from God, and could not; therefore, sin like Adam did. However, some few people such as Noah, Abraham, Isaac, Jacob, and others did receive commands directly from God. On the whole they kept them, but on occasion they also broke them. When they broke them, they had personal sin counted to their charge. But, the death which reigned from Adam to Moses was not only over those who sinned like Adam did, but over those who "had not sinned after the similitude of Adam's transgression", as well, including infants. Therefore, it becomes abundantly clear that physical death is upon mankind because of the sin committed in Adam, and not because of personal actions of sin in this life. It must be recognized, however, that sin in this life may be the immediate cause of death, but not the originating cause. That sin which one may commit in this life which causes his physical death, was sinned as a result of the sinful nature present through the sin in Adam. Therefore, the sin in Adam is the originating cause of all sin and death in mankind.

The last statement of verse fourteen, "who is the figure of him that was to come", refers to Adam being a figure or type of Christ, the one that was to come after Adam. This statement is further explained in the next two verses where explanation is made concerning the eternal second death.

THE SECOND DEATH

But not as the offence, so also is the free gift. For if (since) through the offence of (the) one (the) many be dead (died), much more the grace of (the) God, and the gift by grace, which is by (of) (the) one man, Jesus Christ, hath abounded unto (the) many. And not as it was by (through) one that sinned, so is the gift: for the judgment (indeed) was by (out of) one to (unto) condemnation, but the free gift is of many offences unto justification, (Romans 5:15-16).

The first sentence of verse fifteen, "but not as the offence, so also is the free gift", doesn't make much sense as a sentence until it is carefully thought through. The words "not as" and "so also is" seem to be contradictory thoughts. Actually, they are the keys to understanding the sentence. The sentence is beginning to explain how Adam is a type of Christ, and the remainder of the verse completes the explanation. What Adam did affected all of humanity in an adverse way, and what Christ did affected all of humanity in a favourable way. What Adam and Christ did is "not as" in that they affected mankind in the opposite directions, and what they did is "so also is" in that they both affected all of humanity in the same realm.

The word "if" in the phrase, "for if through the offence of (the) one (the) many be dead," is not a word which questions whether or not the offence of the one man Adam brought eternal death unto the many of humanity, but is what we call the argumentative if, which carries the meaning of "since." The word "many", or literally, "the many" does not refer to a number out of the whole, but to "the many" which makes up the whole of all humanity. We also know that the death spoken of in this verse is the eternal second death, because it is contrasted with the free gift which is eternal life through Christ from the grace of God. So then, Paul is saying that since it is true that the eternal death (separation) is unto the many of mankind because of the one sin in the one man Adam, something else is "much more" powerful or abundant than sin. "Much more the grace of God, and the gift by grace, which is by one man, Jesus Christ, hath abounded unto (the) many." Without all the injected explanatory phrases, he is saying, "much more the grace of God ... hath abounded unto (the) many." How can one truth be "much more" true than another truth? It can't. Neither can the truth spoken of here concerning the grace of God include any more people than is included in the eternal death as a result of the sin in Adam, because it included all mankind and there are no others to include. The only way it can be "much more" is to be more abundant and powerful in its affect upon mankind. In other words, the grace of God which brings life is

32

more abundant and powerful than the sin of Adam which brings death.

What, then, is grace? Simply stated, it is a favor from God toward man which comes from His attribute of love, and which is given without demand or expectation of return. It is a loving favor toward man which he has not earned, merited, or deserved in any way, but extended because of God's love which is gracious.

What, then, is the "gift" which comes by this grace? The gift is eternal life. Note; "For the wages of sin is death; but the gift of God is eternal life through Jesus Christ our Lord," (Romans 6:23). "For by grace are ye saved through faith; and that not of yourselves: it is the gift of God: not of works, lest any man should boast," (Ephesians 2:8-9).

What, then, does "abounded" mean? It means to have more than sufficient, to have an overflowing supply, to have great plenty, to have great quantity, to be very prevalent.

We see then that just as the sin in Adam brought the eternal death unto all mankind, so the grace of God which is greater in power and abundance than sin, has been brought to all mankind in an overflowing supply of great plenty. We see also that along with that grace came the free gift of eternal life which was brought to mankind through the one man, Jesus Christ, who is contrasted with the one man, Adam.

Let us suppose that a Billy Burpo lived in a certain community, and every time he saw a certain minister of the gospel he threw bricks at him, bounced rocks off his head, and mistreated him in general. However, the minister never fought back nor endeavoured to retaliate in any way. Billy continued his actions till one day the minister caught him standing at a corner with his back to a dark alley. The minister quietly sneaked up the alley till he was immediately behind Billy. To his right next to the building was a piece of two-by-four about five feet long. What Billy deserved from the minister was a good "clobbering" with the two-by-four. But, instead of giving Billy what he deserved, the minister took out his billfold, and from it took a thousand dollar bill. With the bill in his hand, he suddenly threw his arms around Billy, holding his arms down to his sides so that Billy could not hit him. While holding Billy in that position, the minister held the thousand dollar bill out in front of Billy and said, "Here, I want to give you this as a gift. I love you." That was grace.

That is what has happened between God and man. Through the sin in Adam, man became separated from God and condemned to the second death, which he deserves. Because of this, man is the natural enemy of God. However, God has said, "Here, I want to give you eternal life as a gift. I love you." That is grace — Grace which is abundant and much more powerful than sin which brought death upon man.

The first phrase of verse sixteen, "and not as it was by one that sinned, so is the gift," is the same as the first sentence of verse fifteen. Note again the words "not as" and "so is." The remainder of the verse again gives further explanation of the phrase which speaks of the likeness and difference of Adam and Christ.

The remainder of verse sixteen states, "for the judgment (indeed) was by one to (unto) condemnation, but the free gift is of many offences unto justification." What is actually stated in the first phrase of that statement should not surprise or startle anyone, but somehow it does, because many people overlook what it says. Notice it again, "for the judgment was by one to (unto) condemnation." "The judgment" speaks of the judgment of mankind by God. The "one" by whom the world of mankind was judged was the one sin committed in the one man Adam. The "condemnation" is the condemnation of all mankind unto the eternal lake of fire which is the second death. Very directly it says that all men are judged and condemned to hell and the eternal lake of fire by the one sin in the one man Adam. No one is a lost condemned hell bound sinner because he lies, cheats, steals, commits adultery, or commits murder. No one is a lost condemned sinner because he sins. The truth is, one sins because he is already a sinner by nature. When one sins he is simply revealing the kind of nature he has. It is very natural for man to sin because he is born with a sinful nature, and retains that sinful nature as long as he is in human flesh. Not only does a man reveal his nature by the way he acts, but all kinds of life reveals its nature by the way it acts. This is true of plant life, animal life, human life, and the Spiritual life of God who lives in the believer. Think it through and see if it is not so.

First of all, let us consider plant life. A man and his wife are taking a stroll through the hills of Virginia in the winter time and come upon an abandoned house and some trees planted in rows. The wife asks her husband what kind of trees they are, because she notices that they are different to other trees. He is able to tell her that they are fruit trees but cannot tell her what kind because he is no tree expert. In the spring of the year, they return to that spot and he is able to tell her that they are apple trees because of the kind of blossoms they produced. At the end of the summer, they return again and he is able to tell her that some are york apple trees, that some are red delicious apple trees, and that others are golden delicious apple trees. He is able to determine this by what the life of the trees have produced. They revealed their nature by what they produced in their life. They did not become apple trees by producing apples, but they produced apples because they were apple trees by nature.

Second, let us consider animal life. As two boys sat on a creek bank fishing, one looked across a field and saw an animal by a pond. As the boys watched the animal and wondered whether it was a dog, a wolf, a coon, a fox, or what it might be, they saw the animal take something in its right paw and walk over to the edge of the pond. The animal then dipped what he had in his paw into the water and then ate it. The boys immediately knew that the animal was a coon. He revealed his nature by the way he acted. He did not become a coon by acting like one, but acted like a coon because he was one by nature.

Thirdly, let us consider human life. When a man sins, he is simply revealing his nature by his actions. He is not becoming a sinner by sinning, but he sins because he is a sinner by nature. It is true that some men sin more than others. However, it takes conscious effort not to sin. Therefore, if anyone should drop his resistance to sin and follow the natural desires and appetites of the flesh, he would become the vilest sinner the world has known. It is natural for a sinful nature to sin.

Fourthly, let us consider spiritual life in man. We see three different men in our community who have had the Holy Spirit of God enter them in regeneration. One of them acts like the other men in the community who are unsaved. The second one is a good Joe and lives a decent and respectable life. The third one is really a dedicated, God fearing, saintly individual. To understand this situation, we must understand that when one is saved, he then has the Divine nature in him in the person of the Holy Spirit, as well as the sinful nature of the natural flesh. Paul said, "For that which I do I allow not: for what I would, that do I not; but what I hate, that do I. If then I do that which I would not, I consent unto the law that it is good. Now then it is no more I that do it, but sin that dwelleth in me," (Romans 7:15-17). He further stated, "For the good that I would I do not: but the evil which I would not, that I do. Now if I do that I would not, it is no more I that do it, but sin that dwelleth in me," (Romans 7:19-20). In concluding the same discussion, Paul said, "So then with the mind I myself serve the law of God; but with the flesh the law of sin," (Romans 7:25). On another occasion, Paul said, "For the flesh lusteth against the Spirit, and the Spirit against the flesh: and these are contrary the one to the other: so that ye cannot do the things that ye would," (Galatians 5:17). Therefore these three men have two natures and they can reveal either nature. The first one is yielding to the nature of the flesh and therefore it is revealed in his actions. The second one is yielding to the Spirit of God just enough to overcome flagrant sin, but not enough for the Holy Spirit to control his life. The third one is doing what all believers should do and yielding himself to the Holy Spirit of God in order that the Godly nature be revealed in his life rather than the sinful fleshly nature. "Walk in (by) the Spirit, and ye shall (should) not (in

no wise) fulfil the lust (desires) of the flesh,"
(Galatians 5:16).

We see, then, that we do not become sinners
by sinning, but that we sin because we have a
sinful nature, and when we sin we are only
revealing the nature which we have. We see
also that we are not judged and condemned to
hell and the eternal lake of fire because of our
personal actions of sin in this life, but that all
mankind is judged and condemned because of
the one sin committed in the one man, Adam.

"But", notice the sharp contrast, "the free
gift is of many offences unto justification."
What a contrast! By the one sin in the one man
Adam all men were judged and condemned, but
through the one free gift of eternal life we are
not only justified in the one sin committed in
Adam, but justified in the many offences which
we have committed as a result of that sin in
Adam as well. Justification is a judicial act in
which God declares the sinner to be righteous.
The meaning of the term can be best understood by an illustration.

Let us suppose that a young couple have a
rural home and that some fellow keeps hanging
around outside the house and singing songs that
are obnoxious to the couple. Becoming totally
disgusted with the fellow, the young husband
walks out of the house with a pistol and shoots
the fellow. The fellow dies immediately, and the
young husband is charged with murder. The
day of the trial comes, the jury hears the
evidence, they weigh it, they make a decision
and pass it on to the judge. The judge pounds
the desk with his gavel and declares "Guilty,
you must hang by your neck until dead." What
the judge has said is that the young man must
suffer the consequences of the wrong he has
done. But let us change the scene. Suppose that

38

young couple is living peacefully until one night he has to go outside and to the back of the house while his wife is sleeping. Presently, a fellow comes down the road and sees the front door open and decides to go in. After entering the house he finds the young lady fast asleep in her bed and decides to shoot her. While he is standing in the doorway taking careful aim, the young husband is quietly coming back in to join his wife in bed. Because he is being quiet so as not to disturb his wife, the intruder doesn't hear him either. Seeing the intruder taking aim to shoot his wife, he quickly but quietly takes his shot gun from the hallway rack and shoots the head from the intruder. He is charged with murder. The day of the trial comes, the jury hears the evidence, they weigh it and make a decision. The decision is passed on to the judge, and he pounds the desk with his gavel and declares "Justified, you may go free." When the judge declared him justified, he was not saying that the young man was not guilty of killing another, but he was saying that the young man could go free and not have to suffer the consequences of what he did. Although he was not innocent or righteous, he was legally and judicially declared to be innocent or righteous so that he would not have to suffer the penalty for what he did. Just so, when God legally declares man justified on the basis of the shed blood of Jesus Christ, He is not saying that man is not a guilty sinner, but that man can go free and not suffer the consequences of sin, which is eternity in the lake of fire. That eternal life which God gives to us as a gift in the place of the eternal death which we deserve, justifies or declares us to be righteous not only from the sin in Adam, but from all the sins we have committed as a result of that sin in Adam.

Now that the condemnation is no longer upon us, neither is the state of spiritual death any longer upon us. The life of God dwells in us in the person of the Holy Spirit instead of being separated from us. This is dealt with in the next verse.

THE SPIRITUAL DEATH

For if by (the) one man's offence (the) death reigned by (through) (the) one; much more they which receive (the) abundance of (the) grace and of the gift of (the) righteousness shall reign in life by (through) (the) one, Jesus Christ, (Romans 5:17).

Notice that the spiritual death reigned or had authority by the one sin in the one man Adam. We know that the death spoken of here is the spiritual death because it is contrasted with the spiritual life. Notice that the "gift of righteousness" is received through receiving the abundant grace that is offered. Is a man righteous after he is saved? No! The righteousness which he has is a gift which has been given to him from God, Who is on the outside. It is Christ in him in the person of the Holy Spirit. The righteousness of Jesus Christ is the only righteousness acceptable to God. Our own will not suffice. When we "receive (the) abundance of (the) grace and of the gift of (the) righteousness", which is Christ in us in the person of the Holy Spirit through regeneration, then we are no longer in a state of spiritual death (separated from God by the Spirit of God leaving man), but in a state of spiritual life, and "shall reign in life by (through) (the) one, Jesus Christ." We shall reign in life instead of death because the Spirit of life which is more powerful than the spirit of death is within us.

Once we have received the Holy Spirit in regeneration, we are no longer spiritually dead. Once we are no longer spiritually dead, the Spirit of God who is in us has saved us from the condemnation of the second death and sealed us till the day or redemption. Once He has sealed us, we are assured of the resurrection of our body at His coming.

Thus far, we have seen the introduction of death in verse twelve; the physical death which is upon man because of the sin in Adam, in verses thirteen and fourteen; the condemnation of the second death which is unto man because of the sin in Adam, in verses fifteen and sixteen; and the spiritual death which is upon man because of the sin in Adam, in verse seventeen. In the remainder of the chapter, verses eighteen through twenty-one, we will see a further explanation concerning death, and note that man did not do anything to become a lost condemned sinner, and that he cannot do anything to become righteous, justified, saved.

THE DELIVERANCE FROM DEATH

Therefore as by (through) the (one) offence of one judgment came upon (unto) all men to (unto) condemnation; even so by (through) the righteousness of one the free gift came upon (unto) all men unto justification of life. For as by (through) (the) one man's disobedience (the) many were made (constituted) sinners, so by (through) the obedience of (the) one shall (the) many be made (constituted) righteous. Moreover the law entered (came, was given), that the offence might abound. But where sin abounded, (the) grace did much more abound (exceedingly abounded): that as (the) sin hath

41

reigned unto (in) (the) death, even so might (the) grace reign through righteousness unto eternal life by (through) Jesus Christ our Lord,(Romans 5:18-21).

These verses of explanation may also be divided into three parts: condemnation and justification, in verse eighteen; the sinners and the righteous, in verse nineteen; and, the abounding sin and the super abounding grace, in verses twenty and twenty-one.

THE CONDEMNATION AND THE JUSTIFICATION

Therefore as by the offence of one judgment came upon (unto) all men to (unto) condemnation; even so by the righteousness of one the free gift came upon (unto) all men unto justification of life, (Romans 5:18).

If there was any doubt left in the mind of any reader after reading the exposition of verse sixteen as to whether or not it is true that man is lost and condemned by the sin committed in Adam instead of by personal actions of sin committed in this present life, then the first part of verse eighteen should expell such doubt. Notice that "by the offence of one judgment came upon (unto) all men to (unto) condemnation." It could not be stated with any more clarity or definiteness. All men are judged and condemned to hell and the eternal lake of fire by the one sin in the one man Adam. It must be repeated; no man is a lost, judged, condemned, hell bound sinner because of what he does, but because of what he is by nature through the sin in Adam.

"Even so" or "so also" indicates a

comparison instead of a contrast. A contrast is definitely seen in the second half of the verse with the first half, but the emphasis is upon the likeness, "even so." "Even so by the righteousness of one the free gift came upon (unto) all men unto justification of life." Just as it is true that all men have a judgment unto condemnation because of the one sin committed in Adam, so it is also true that all men have a free gift unto justification because of the righteousness in Christ. Since this is a Scriptural statement, it must be true. However, it must be clearly understood what is not said and what is said. It does not say that all men are condemned and therefore will spend an eternity in the lake of fire, nor does it say that all men have the free gift of righteousness and therefore justified before God. What it does say is that because of the sin in Adam, a judgment has come "unto" all men "unto" condemnation. It also says that because of the righteousness of Christ, as opposed to the sin of Adam, the free gift of eternal life has come "unto" all men "unto" justification of life. In other words, because of the sin in Adam, God judged mankind and pronounced a condemnation of man "unto" (motion toward) the eternal lake of fire. All men are headed for the condemnation pronounced, and will enter into it if physical death takes them before they accept the redemption provided for them in Christ. Just as they have been judged "unto" condemnation by the sin in the one man Adam, so by the righteousness or righteous act of Christ in which He died for mankind upon the cross, the free gift of eternal life which is a redemption from the eternal lake of fire, came "unto" (motion toward) all men which is "unto" justification of life itself. Just as it is true that all men have been judged unto condemnation, but that all are not in the condemnation, so it is also true that all men have eternal life provided for them, but that all men are not partakers of eternal life. Notice the words of Christ. In speaking to Nicodemus, He said,

For God so loved the world, that he gave his only begotten Son, that whosoever believeth in him should not perish, but have everlasting life. For God sent not his Son into the world to condemn the world; but that the world through him might be saved. He that believeth on him is not condemned: but he that believeth not is condemned already, because he hath not believed in the name of the only begotten Son of God, (John 3:16-18).

In writing to Titus, Paul said,

For the grace of God that bringeth salvation hath appeared to all men, Teaching us that, denying ungodliness and worldly lusts, we should live soberly, righteously, and godly, in this present world; Looking for that blessed hope, and the glorious appearing of the great God and our Saviour Jesus Christ; Who gave himself for us, that he might redeem us from all iniquity, and purify unto himself a peculiar people, zealous of good works, (Titus 2:11-14).

Before leaving verse eighteen, we must notice three other things. First, a man does not become a literal, physical part of the all men who are judged and condemned, till birth, the physical birth. Just so, a man does not become a part of the all men who have received the free gift of eternal life unto justification till the spiritual birth takes place. Second, once a man has become a partaker of the gift of eternal life through the rebirth of the Spirit in him, he is not only justified or declared righteous in the sin committed in Adam and the many offences committed as a result of it, as is indicated in verse sixteen, but is also justified in all of life itself. "The free gift came upon (unto) all men unto justification of life." Third, it must be noticed that man did not do anything personally in this present life to make him lost and condemned, and he did not do anything personally to make himself saved from that condemnation and justified before God.

This third point is further explained and clarified in verse nineteen.

THE SINNERS AND THE RIGHTEOUS

For as by (through)(the) one man's disobedience (the) many were made (constituted) sinners, so by (through) the obedience of (the) one shall (the) many be made (constituted) righteous, (Romans 5:19).

The statement that the many of mankind were constituted sinners by "the one man's disobedience" is clear. The one man, of course, is Adam. It is obvious that my disobedience could not make all others of mankind sinners. Therefore, the one man can be none other than Adam. It should be clear, then, that one does not become a sinner by committing sins of any kind in this present physical life, regardless of how hideous they may be, but that one is a sinner because of the one sin committed in the one man Adam. Just so, the second statement of the verse is just as clear in stating that mankind may be constituted righteous by "the

45

obedience of the one." That one, of course, is none other than Jesus Christ. Even if a man could be righteous through his own obedience, it is obvious that his obedience could not make "the many" of mankind righteous. Therefore, "the obedience of the one" could speak of none other than Jesus Christ.

Notice three facts which clearly stand out in this verse. First, no man is made a sinner in God's sight by sinning, but is a sinner because of the sin in Adam. Second, no man is declared righteous or justified in God's sight because of his personal obedience, but because of the obedience of Christ, in which He was obedient to the will of the Father to die upon the cross. "And being found in fashion as a man, he humbled himself, and became obedient unto death, even the death of the cross," (Philippians 2:8). Third, it must logically follow that if a person did not do any personal act of sin in this life in order to make himself become a sinner before God, and therefore lost; and if a person did not do any personal act of obedience or righteousness in this life in order to make himself righteous or justified before God, and therefore saved; then he could not commit any personal action of sin to make him lose his salvation. Stating it another way, we might ask, since a man did not do anything to become a sinner and didn't do anything to become saved, then how could he do anything to become lost again? More directly, we might ask, how could a man lose his salvation by personal actions when he wasn't saved by personal actions nor lost in the first place by personal actions? The answer is obvious. One cannot be lost again once he has been saved. Once a man makes a decision to accept the atoning work of Jesus Christ for his redemption from the penalty of sin, that decision is irrevocable. We must recognize that our present salvation is not from sinning, but from the condemnation of sin, the eternal lake of fire, which is upon us because of the sin in Adam. Our souls and spirits are saved, sealed, and secured for eternity in glory the instant the Holy Spirit enters us in the regeneration. However, the body is only assured of its redemption from the presence of sin in the future when Christ comes to take His own to be with Him.

THE ABOUNDING SIN AND THE SUPER ABOUNDING GRACE

Moreover the law entered (came, was given), that the offence might abound. But where sin abounded, (the) grace did much more abound (exceedingly abounded): that as (the) sin hath reigned unto (in) (the) death, even so might (the) grace reign through righteousness unto eternal life by (through) Jesus Christ our Lord, (Romans 5:20-21).

The first brief sentence in this section perplexes many. "Moreover the law entered (came, was given), that the offence might abound." You mean that God gave the law to Moses so that there would be more sin? you may ask. Yes! We must always keep in mind the fact that God did not give the law to be kept, but to be broken. It was not given as a means of saving man, but as a means of condemning man. When God gave the law, He knew that it was impossible for man to keep it and did not intend for man to keep it. Remember what Paul said in verse thirteen? "For until the law sin was in the world: but sin is not imputed when there is no law," (Romans 5:13). Mankind was doing wrong in the sight of God before He gave the law to Moses, but man did not have his actions of sins counted against him because there was no law. Once the law was given, man's actions of sins that were counted against him "abounded." He was not doing any more wrong in the sight of God than he was doing before the law was given, but he had more actions of sins counted to his charge because he had a command from God concerning right and wrong. The law reflected God's standard of holiness. That standard of holiness did not come into existence at the time God gave the law to Moses, but was only revealed to man at that time. God had that same standard of holiness throughout all eternity past, and will have the same standard of holiness throughout all eternity future. God does not and cannot change.

After the law was given, man knew God's standard of holiness. Observing God's standard of holiness and observing his own life, man was able to recognize that he was unlike God, and therefore unholy because God is holy. Once man recognized through the law that he was unlike God and therefore unholy, he was able to realize that he was unholy by nature, because all life reveals its nature by the way it acts. He was not acting the way God acted, so he knew that his nature was different. The law, then, showed to him his lost, sinful, condemned state and nature and pointed him to his need for salvation. In reference to this fact, Paul said, "The strength of sin is the law," (I Corinthians 15:56).

Now we know that what things soever the law saith, it saith to them who are under the law:

48

that every mouth may be stopped, and all the world may become guilty before God. Therefore by the deeds of the law there shall no flesh be justified in his sight: for by the law is the knowledge of sin, (Romans 3:19-20).

But the scripture hath concluded all under sin, that the promise by faith of Jesus Christ might be given to them that believe. But before faith came, we were kept under the law, shut up unto the faith which should afterwards be revealed. Wherefore the law was our schoolmaster to bring us unto Christ, that we might be justified by faith, (Galatians 3:22-24).

We see, then, that the law was not given so that man would actually sin more, but that he might have more of his natural sins counted against him, and thereby recognize his need and turn to God to find a solution for his need, which is found in the person of Jesus Christ.

"But where sin abounded, grace did much more abound." What a contrast! In verse fifteen we are told that the sin in Adam brought death to the many of mankind, but that the grace of God which gives life and which is more powerful than death abounded unto the many of mankind. But here we are told that the sins which man has counted against him have abounded, and that the grace of God which justifies or declares man righteous in sin has much more or exceedingly abounded. That is, the grace of God has abounded much more than all of man's sin. No one can sin so much or so often nor badly enough but what God's grace isn't sufficient to cover it. Thank God for such great grace which is so much greater than our sin!

Why did God extend such grace? "That as

(the) sin hath reigned unto (in) (the) death, even so might grace reign through righteousness unto eternal life by (through) Jesus Christ our Lord," (Romans 5:21). Briefly stated, God's grace abounded more than man's sin so that His grace could reign unto eternal life, like the sin in Adam reigned unto eternal death. Notice particularly that "the sin" reigned or had authority unto or in "the death", but that "the grace" reigned or had authority through the righteousness of Jesus Christ our Lord unto "eternal life." Since, then, the grace of God is more abundant than sin, then His grace is sufficient to save all and to cause all to have eternal life reigning over them instead of eternal death.

For other expositions of Romans 5:12-21, see the works listed in the footnote below.*

What we have observed in Romans 5:12-21, is twofold. First, man is lost and condemned because of his sin in Adam, and he is saved from the condemnation by the righteous act of Christ. Second, man is saved from the condemnation which is upon him because of the sin in Adam, but is not saved from sinning. While it has been clearly explained what makes a person lost and what makes a person saved, nothing has been said about how one may appropriate that gift or have God's grace affectively applied to him. In simpler terms, we

* Augustus H. Strong, *Systematic Theology,* The Judson Press, Philadelphia, 1960, pp:625-627.

William R. Newell, *Romans Verse by Verse,* Moody Press, Chicago, 1938, pp:176-198.

Marvin R. Vincent, *Word Studies in the New Testament,* Vol. III, Wm. B. Eerdmans Publishing Company, Grand Rapids, 1969, pp: 62-65.

W. Robertson Nicoll, Editor, *The Expositors Greek Testament,* Vol. II, Wm. B. Eerdmans Publishing Company, Grand Rapids, 1970, pp: 627-631.

have not yet been told how an individual may personally receive the gift of eternal life and thereby be saved from hell and the eternal lake of fire.

"For the wages of (the) sin is death; but the (free) gift of (the) God is eternal life through (in) Jesus Christ our Lord," (Romans 6:23). Note the first statement, "for the wages of the sin is death." A wage is something that is earned and deserved. "The sin" refers to the sin in Adam. We know that "death" speaks of the eternal second death because it is contrasted with the eternal life. The wages of a week's work might be two hundred dollars. What one earns and deserves for working a week is two hundred dollars. In the same way, the wages of the sin is death. What man has earned and deserved by the sin he committed in Adam is eternal death in the lake of fire. "But", notice the sharp contrast, "the free gift of God is eternal life." A gift is something which is given with no strings or conditions attached. Suppose a pastor should declare, "I am giving a free gift of one hundred dollars to everyone who is at Sunday School on time next week and then stays for Church." Is he really offering a "free gift"? No! He is offering a bribe. Suppose someone should say to you, "I have a free gift of one thousand dollars to give to you, but I want you to polish my shoes at least one time." Is he really offering a "free gift"? No! He is offering very high wages but not a gift. The motive for giving is love. The person who gives a gift is the one who pays for it, and then freely gives it because he wants to do so. We do not ask for gifts. Something which has been given in answer to a request is not a gift. A gift is that which is paid for by the giver, and given out of his own volition because he wants the recipient to have it. The giving is motivated by love, not merit or request. A gift, then, is something which is given with no strings attached, and something which the recipient may take and freely use as if he purchased or earned it himself.

The person giving the "free gift" in this case is God. It is not being given by Jesus Christ, the Holy Spirit, the church, the pastor, the priest, the rabbi, or anyone else. It is "the free gift of God." The free gift which God is offering and giving to all who will receive it is "eternal life." God, in His mercy and grace, instead of paying us the wage we have earned and deserved, which is eternal death in the lake of fire, is offering us a gift which we have not earned or deserved, which is eternal life to be lived forever in heavenly bliss. The eternal life that He offers is through or in "Jesus Christ our Lord." Since the eternal life He offers is in Christ, then we must receive Christ in order to have eternal life. Christ is in the believer in the person of the Holy Spirit when the Holy Spirit enters in regeneration and saves the person from the state of spiritual death and the condemnation of the second death. We have already learned this truth previously, but how can one know that he has received the Holy Spirit in the new birth and therefore been saved? The simple answer is, "by faith." "For by grace are ye saved through faith; and that not of yourselves (the saving is not of yourself): it (the salvation) is the gift of God: Not of works, lest any man should boast," (Ephesians 2:8-9). At this point it becomes clear that one is saved by God's grace, but it has not yet been made clear what one is to place his faith in, in order to receive "the gift of God" which is "eternal life."

The object of one's faith by which he can know that he has been saved and received eternal life is also presented to us by Paul in the book of Romans. "That if thou shalt confess with thy mouth the Lord Jesus, and shalt believe in thine heart that God hath raised Him from (from among) the dead (ones), thou shalt be saved," (Romans 10:9). Since this verse tells how "thou shalt be saved," then it would behoove us to examine it closely. The first phrase, "that if thou shalt confess," could well be rendered in modern English as, "that if you will confess." The word confess hinders the understanding of many because it has come to be associated with bad things only, such as confessing sins, confessing crimes, etc. However, the word simply means to admit. One may admit to something bad or to something good. In this case we are asked to admit with our mouth something good, that our Lord is Jesus. At this point a very logical and legitimate question may be asked. How can one say that Jesus is his Lord, which means master and owner, when he knows that by his very nature he is a child of the devil and condemned to the lake of fire? When one knows that he has been "sold under sin" and by nature belongs to Satan, how can he say that Jesus owns him? Actually, to admit that Jesus is our Lord, is to admit that He died for us upon the cross, and that He shed His blood there for us in order to pay the price of redemption and buy us back from the power of sin, Satan, and the condemnation. Since, then, He paid the price to buy us, He owns us and is therefore our master and owner.

Forasmuch as ye know that ye were not redeemed with corruptible things, as silver and gold, from your vain conversation received by tradition from your fathers; But with the precious blood of Christ, as of a lamb without blemish and without spot, (I Peter 1:18-19).

And they sung a new song, saying, Thou art worthy to take the book, and to open the seals thereof: for thou wast slain, and hast redeemed us to God by thy blood out of every kindred, and tongue, and people, and nation, (Revelation 5:9). (For further explanation on the death of Christ, see Appendix A).

Therefore, we are told that if we would admit with our mouth that Jesus is our Lord because He shed His blood for us on the cross in order to buy us back from the condemnation, and believe one other thing, we would be saved. We are told to "believe in thine heart that God hath raised Him (Jesus) from the dead (and) thou shalt be saved." To be saved, then, one must believe and admit that Jesus is his Lord, and have confidence that the Biblical statement that God raised Jesus from among the dead ones after He died for us is absolutely true. Notice the statement "believe in thine heart." This word "heart" is used many times in the New Testament in the place of "mind", and in this instance could not refer to the organ that pumps blood through our body, because we do not think with our literal heart. To believe in the heart is to allow what you believe to move you to depend upon or act upon it.

You have a friend who works at hard labour for sixty hours each week for a dollar per hour. In talking with him one day, you tell him where he can get a job working only thirty hours per week that pays ten dollars per hour. The organization is large and will hire anyone who does not have a job, but will not discuss employment with anyone who is already employed. Suppose, now, that your friend goes back to his old job each day and talks to the other workers about what you told him. He says that he believes what you said, and complains about the hard work and low pay, but never acts upon what you told him. This would indicate that he had a head knowledge and understanding of what you told him, but that he did not have enough confidence in your word to act upon it. But, suppose that instead of going back to his old job after you told him of the new opportunity, he got up the next morning and put on dress clothes and went to his employer and said, "I quit, I want my termination papers." On the strength of your word alone, he quit his job and went to the new place fully expecting to get the job you told him about. That would be placing confidence in your word. That would be exercising faith in your word. That would be believing in the heart.

If anyone would be saved, then, he must believe and admit that Jesus died for him upon the cross and shed His blood there in order to redeem or buy him back from the condemnation of sin, and have confidence in the fact that God raised Jesus from among the dead ones after He died for him. Having believed these things, one has the promise of God to rely upon and can thereby know that he is saved because God promised him that he would be if he only believed what He told him. Once one exercises his confidence or faith in that promise of God, he is saved. "For by grace are ye saved through faith," (Ephesians 2:8). Jesus said, "He that believeth on him (Jesus, the Son of God) is not condemned: but he that believeth not is condemned already, because he hath not believed in the name of the only begotten Son of God," (John 3:18).

Summarily stated, God has said that if anyone would place his confidence in the death, burial, and literal bodily resurrection of Jesus, he would be saved. However, there are many people who believe these things who are saved, and many people who believe these things who are not saved. This may appear to be a contradiction, but is not. Those who believe these things and are saved, are saved because they have confidence in the Word of God to believe that they are saved just because they believe them. Those who believe these things and are not saved, are not saved because they have not placed a confidence or faith in the Word of God, to believe that they are saved just because they believe these things. Once they simply believe what God said is actually true, they are immediately saved "by grace through faith." We must not become confused concerning what saves a person. A person's faith does not save him. The grace of God saves, but one enters into that grace which is made available to all through faith. "Therefore being justified by faith, we have peace with God through our Lord Jesus Christ: By whom also we have access by faith into this grace wherein we stand, and rejoice in hope of the glory of God," (Romans 5:1-2). This is exactly what happened to Abraham, and we are told that the same can happen to us.

He staggered not at the promise of God through unbelief; but was strong in faith, giving glory to God; And being fully persuaded that, what he had promised, he was able also to perform. And therefore it was imputed to him for righteousness. Now it was not written for his sake alone, that it was imputed to him; But for us also, to whom it shall be imputed, if we believe on him that raised up Jesus our Lord from the dead; Who was delivered for our offences, and was raised again for our justification, (Romans 4:20-25). (For further explanation and assurance of salvation by simply believing God, see Appendix B).

CHAPTER II

WHAT ONE SHOULD KNOW ABOUT BAPTISM

CHAPTER II

WHAT ONE SHOULD KNOW

ABOUT BAPTISM

The first act of obedience which one should perform after being saved is that of baptism. A christian baptism is the immersion of a believer in water in token of regeneration by a Scripturally authorized administrator.

THE DEFINITION OF BAPTISM

The word "baptize" comes from the Greek word, "baptizo." It is not a translation into the English language, but a transliteration. The Greek word "baptizo" is transferred to the English by simply changing the "o" at the end of the word to an "e" so that it will have an English sound and appearance. Thus, the meaning is not conveyed in the English. The Greek word "baptizo", means to make whelmed. The word "baptizo", comes from the verb, "bapto", which means to whelm or to cover wholly. The English word "whelm" means to submerge, to engulf, to utterly overcome, or to overwhelm. Therefore, to "baptize" one in water would mean to cover wholly, to submerge, to engulf, or to utterly overcome with water.

Some form of the word for baptize is found in the Greek New Testament at least one hundred and fifteen times. All but four times it is rendered as baptize in the English. In Mark 7:4, it is translated as "wash", and a form of it in the same verse is translated as "washing." In Luke 11:38, it is translated as "washed", and in Hebrews 9:10, a form of it is translated as "washings." In all four cases, the idea conveyed is not that of washing, as we ordinarily think of washing, but that of dipping. Therefore, the idea of submerging is always intended when any form of the Greek word for baptize is used.

In some circles it is commonly believed and taught that the words for washing and baptizing are used interchangeably in the New Testament. However, an examination of the Greek text reveals that this is not true. While it is true that the word for "baptize" is rendered as "wash" four times in the New Testament, the two Greek words which mean "to wash" are never rendered as baptize. When words are used interchangeably, the first is used in the place of the second, and the second is used in the place of the first. This is not found to be true with the words for "wash" and "baptize." The word for "baptize" is rendered with the idea of "washing" four times in the English, but the two words for "washing" are never rendered as "baptize" in the English. Furthermore, the four times that the word for "baptize" is rendered in the English as "wash", the idea conveyed is that of dipping into so that the thing dipped is submerged. The meaning of the word "baptize", then, is to dip into, to submerge, to engulf, to completely cover.

THE MODE OF BAPTISM

Once the definition of the word has been settled in one's mind, the mode of baptism is also settled. From the definition of the Greek word, it can be readily seen that the mode of baptism is that of dipping or submerging one into water so that the one being baptized is engulfed or completely covered with water. Therefore, the proper mode is that of immersion.

Perchance there is doubt in the mind of anyone concerning the definition and mode of baptism, it may be well to examine a Scriptural account of the act. In the book of Acts, we have the account of the conversion and baptism of the Ethiopian eunuch.

Then Philip opened his mouth, and began at the same scripture, and preached unto him Jesus. And as they went on their way, they came unto a certain water: and the eunuch said, See, here is water; what doth hinder me to be baptized? And Philip said, If thou believest with all thine heart, thou mayest. And he answered and said, I believe that Jesus Christ is the Son of God. And he commanded the chariot to stand still: and they went down both into the water, both Philip and the eunuch; and he baptized him. And when they were come up out of the water, the Spirit of the Lord caught away Philip, that the eunuch saw him no more: and he went on his way rejoicing, (Acts 8:35-39).

From this record we have two ways of knowing that the proper mode of baptism is immersion. First, he could have been baptized before coming to the oasis if the mode of sprinkling or pouring water over his head could have been used. This fact is readily obvious because they were on the Gaza desert, and no one would cross the Gaza desert without a supply of water. Therefore, a small amount of that water supply could have been used for the baptism instead of waiting till they came to a pond of water, if baptism did not have to be by immersion. Secondly, it is recorded that Philip, who was doing the baptizing, and the eunuch, who was being baptized, both went down into the water; "and they went down both into the water, both Philip and the eunuch; and he baptized him." The fact that they both went "down into" the water indicates that the baptism was by immersion. If the baptism of the eunuch had been by sprinkling or by pouring, then neither of them would have had to have gone "down into" the water. In fact, they would not have had to stepped into the edge of the water at all, because standing by the edge would have been sufficient.

We see, then, by the definition of the word and by the description of the action that the proper mode of baptism is immersion in water.

THE SUBJECT OF BAPTISM

From the above quoted Scripture portion from the book of Acts, it can be readily seen that the proper subject of baptism is one who has professed faith in Jesus Christ for salvation. The eunuch, seeing the water, asked Philip what hindered him from being baptized. Philip answered, "If thou believest with all thine heart, thou mayest." What Philip told the eunuch was basically this; that he could not be baptized until he placed his confidence in the death, burial, and resurrection of Jesus Christ for his salvation. The eunuch expressed such faith when he said to Philip, "I believe that Jesus Christ is the Son of God." After he assured Philip that he believed, then Philip went down into the water with him and baptized him.

Throughout the Scriptural record, wherever there is an account of water baptism, the baptism is always of one who has already professed personal faith in Christ unto salvation. On the day of Pentecost when Peter preached and many were saved, baptism followed; "Then they that gladly received his word were baptized," (Acts 2:41). The Apostle Paul was saved and then baptized three days later, (Acts 9:3-6,9,17-18). The household of Cornelius was saved and then baptized, (Acts 10:44-48). Therefore, the proper subject of baptism is one who has already been saved through personal faith in Jesus Christ.

Baptism, then, is the immersion of a believer in water. This would mean, therefore, that one who had been immersed in water before he was saved, did not experience a christian baptism, because the immersion he submitted to was that of an unbeliever instead of the immersion of a believer in water.

THE MEANING OF BAPTISM

Baptism is not just a religious ritual to be performed, but a meaningful act through which the one being baptized is showing to the world in symbol what Jesus Christ did to secure his redemption, and to show forth his own identification with the death, burial, and resurrection of Christ which was performed on his behalf. Therefore, its meaning is three-fold.

First, it shows forth what Jesus Christ did in order to save mankind. This fact is seen in the baptism of Jesus Himself.

Then cometh Jesus from Galilee to Jordan unto John, to be baptized of him. But John forbad him, saying, I have need to be baptized of thee, and comest thou to me? And Jesus answering said unto him, Suffer it to be so now: for thus it becometh us to fulfil all righteousness. Then he suffered him, (Matthew 3:13-15).

In order to understand the purpose of the baptism of Jesus, we must closely examine the statement which Jesus made to John in verse fifteen. "Suffer (allow, permit) it to be so now: for thus it becometh (it is suitable or proper for) us to fulfill (furnish, satisfy, execute, finish, verify, coincide with) all righteousness (equity, justification)." Simply stated, the verse says, "Allow it to be so now: for thus it is proper for us to coincide with all righteousness or justification." Jesus told John that He should be baptized by him because it was suitable or proper for them to do that thing which coincides with all righteousness. All righteousness and justification is in Jesus Christ, and in being baptized, He was showing forth in a proper or suitable form what He was going to do in order to save man that he might be justified in Him. When He was baptized by John, He was showing forth in symbol that He was going to die, be buried, and be raised again in order to secure man's redemption and justification. Therefore, when a believer is baptized, he is showing forth in a symbol what Christ did to redeem and justify him.

Secondly, it is to show forth in a symbol that the one being baptized has identified himself with the death, burial, and resurrection of Christ and accepted it as a substitutionary work for himself.

Know ye not, that so many of us as were baptized into Jesus Christ were baptized into his death? Therefore we are buried with him by baptism into death: that like as Christ was raised up from the dead by the glory of the Father, even so we also should walk in newness of life. For if we have been planted together in the likeness of his death, we shall be also in the likeness of his resurrection: Knowing this, that our old man is crucified with him, that the body of sin might be destroyed, that henceforth we should not serve sin, (Romans 6:3-6).

Thirdly, it is to show one's willingness to submit himself in obedience to his Lord's command. Just before ascending into heaven after His resurrection, Jesus said to His disciples, "All power is given unto me in heaven and in earth. Go ye therefore, and teach (disciple) all nations, baptizing them in the name of the Father, and of the Son, and of the Holy Ghost (Spirit)," (Matthew 28:18-19). Since He commanded the disciples to baptize all who would become disciples, it is obvious that He intended that those who became disciples should submit to baptism. Therefore, baptism is an act of obedience on the part of the believer to the Lord who bought him.

From the foregoing facts, it is obvious that one is not baptized in order to be saved, but because he has already been saved. Baptism is in token of regeneration. So, baptism is the immersion of a believer in water in token of regeneration.

THE ADMINISTRATOR OF BAPTISM

Among conservatives there is very little disagreement on the subject of baptism until they come to the question of who has the authority to baptize. Some believe that it doesn't matter who does the baptizing, even if he or she is an atheist, just so long as the person being baptized is being baptized for the right purpose and with the right intent and motive.

Others believe that any believer has the authority to baptize a new convert at any time. There are others who believe that any God called ordained minister has the right and authority to baptize new converts. There are still others who believe that only a local church has the authority to baptize. There are even those who believe that only a local church of a particularly named denomination of churches has the authority to baptize. Last of all, some believe that only a pastor who was baptized by a pastor who was baptized by a pastor who was baptized by Jesus, who was baptized by John the Baptist, and who is a pastor of a particular brand of local church which has authorized him to do so has the authority to baptize.

We cannot determine which position is right by finding the most popular position, by listing the names of great men of God who have embraced and practiced a particular position, or by studying church history; but by examining the commission given by Jesus and determining to whom He gave the commission and authority to baptize.

Then the eleven disciples went away into Galilee, into a mountain where Jesus had appointed them. And when they saw him, they worshipped him: but some doubted. And Jesus came and spake unto them, saying, All power is given unto me in heaven and in earth. Go ye therefore, and teach all nations, baptizing them in the name of the Father, and of the Son, and of the Holy Ghost: Teaching them to observe all things whatsoever I have commanded you: and, lo, I am with you alway, even unto the end of the world. Amen, (Matthew 28:16-20).

This portion of Scripture is commonly

referred to as the great commission. It is also commonly stated that the great commission was given to the church. However, there is a difference of opinion concerning the meaning and usage of the word "church." The meaning and usage of the word "church" in the New Testament is rather clear, however. It is because of modern day thought patterns concerning the church that the differences exists. (See chapter three, and Appendix C, for a detailed study of the word "church"). The word which is rendered "church" in the New Testament should more literally be rendered "assembly." Therefore, if the commission was given to the assembly, the authority to baptize was obviously given to the local churches or assemblies. It behooves us, then, to study the commission and see if we can determine to whom it was given.

Let us suppose first of all, that the authority to baptize was given to anyone, saved or unsaved. If this were true, then the unsaved not only have a commission to baptize, but also to disciple all nations and teach the Word of God to all new converts. This, of course, is ridiculous. The unsaved have no more authority to baptize than they do to preach the gospel and teach the Word.

Secondly, let us suppose that any saved person has the authority to baptize. If this is true, then every saved person also has the commission to preach the gospel to every nation of the world, and to teach the converts. We know that this cannot be the true position because God chooses certain men and calls them to minister His Word, and because it is not possible for every christian to go into every nation of the world to preach the gospel and teach the Word of God. Our Lord does not command us to do what cannot be done. This position, then, is almost as ridiculous as the first position.

The third position, which states that any God called ordained minister has the authority to baptize because the commission was given to the eleven apostles, is far more feasible than the first two positions, but is seemingly still lacking when examined. If the commission was given to the eleven apostles only, then the commission would have ceased when the apostles died, unless we admit to an apostolic succession. This would mean that only the ministers have the authority and understanding to teach the Word of God. We deny the Church of Rome the right to an apostolic succession, why; then, should we claim it for ourselves? This position, then, is also unreasonable.

Fourthly, let us suppose that only a local church has the authority to baptize. Since a local church is an assembly of Scripturally baptized people who have assembled in obedience to the command of Christ, this position seems very feasible. The eleven were saved and baptized, and had assembled in obedience to the command of Christ at the place He had appointed for them. "Then the eleven disciples went away into Galilee, into a mountain where Jesus had appointed them," (Matthew 28:16). Therefore, they constituted a New Testament church or assembly. To this assembly, He said, "All power (authority) is given unto me in heaven and in earth. Go ye therefore, and teach (disciple) all nations, baptizing them in the name of the Father, and of the Son, and of the Holy Ghost (Spirit): teaching them to observe all things whatsoever I have commanded you: and, lo, I am with you alway, even unto the end of the world. Amen,"

(Matthew 28:18-20). This commission is impossible when placed in the context of any of the three preceding positions. However, when we consider it in the context of the position now under consideration, it is not only possible but very logical. Since Jesus has had all power or authority in heaven and in earth given to Him, He, by that authority has commissioned the church or assemblies to go forth in His name. Whereas every individual believer or preacher cannot go into every nation to make disciples and teach, the church can. The commission would have ceased with the death of the apostles had it been given to them, but since it was given to the local church or churches (assemblies), it will never cease, because the church will not cease. As the older members of a congregation depart from their bodies to go to be with their Lord, new believers are being added to the assembly. Therefore it never ceases. The Lord could not be with each believer or preacher till the end of the age to aid them in the work of the commission, because they do not live throughout the age, but He could be with a local church or the local churches which will be here till the end of the age. This position, then, seems to be the most feasible of all, which means that a local church has the authority to baptize.

The fifth position, which states that only a local church with a particular denominational name has the right to baptize, readily becomes untenable when one realizes that this position makes a name the determining factor as to whether or not a local assembly is a New Testament church, instead of the doctrinal position held by the assembly.

The sixth position is even more untenable than the fifth, because it not only makes a name the determining factor as to whether an assembly is a New Testament church or not, but also claims an apostolic succession for itself which can not be substantiated by Scripture nor by church history.

The only reasonable position is the fourth, which states that only a local church has the authority to baptize. Since the great commission was given to a local church, then the local church has the authority to administer baptism. Since the church has the authority of Christ to baptize, then the assembly may choose any man from its number to administer baptism to a new convert. That authority, however, is usually given to the pastor by a vote of the church congregation. In most churches the vote is cast one time and a statement of the vested authority is written in the church constitution stating that the pastor is authorized to baptize new converts. In some few churches, a vote is cast each time someone is to be baptized, and the authority to administer it is given to the pastor or some other male believer.

A scripturally authorized administrator of baptism, then, is one who has been authorized to baptize a new convert by a local church or assembly, which was given the authority to do so by Christ. In concluding this chapter on baptism, we must repeat the definition of baptism which was given at the beginning of the chapter, and which has been explained phrase by phrase throughout the chapter. A christian baptism is the immersion of a believer in water in token of regeneration by a scripturally authorized administrator.

CHAPTER III
WHAT ONE SHOULD KNOW ABOUT THE CHURCH

CHAPTER III

WHAT ONE SHOULD KNOW ABOUT THE CHURCH

Much has been said and written about the church, but there is much more which needs to be said from a Scriptural viewpoint. However, the purpose of this chapter is not to give a thorough treatise on the church, but to give a few basic facts concerning the church in order that one might know what it is, what it is not, and what one's relationship to the church should be.

THE DEFINITION OF A CHURCH

The word "church" is commonly used to refer to the total body of all believers. However, the Scriptural usage of the word is in reference to a local assembly of baptized believers in one place who have voluntarily united together in organization with elected leaders and officers for the purpose of glorifying God according to the teachings of the Bible. The New Testament emphasis is upon such local groups of believers as is evidenced by the meaning of the Greek word "ekklasia", which is translated "church", and by the contextual usage of the word in the New Testament. (For an analysis of each time the word for church, ekklasia, appears, see Appendix C).

Having formulated a definition of the word "church", we should break it down and examine it phrase by phrase. Note first of all

that a church is a local assembly of baptized
believers in one place. Since the meaning of the
Greek word "ekklasia" is primarily
"assembly", then it is obvious that the
assembly must be of believers in one given
local area, because all believers cannot
assemble together in one place till the rapture.
We have already seen in chapter two, that one
cannot be baptized till after he has been saved.
At the time of salvation, one is "baptized" or
placed into a new relationship with Christ by
the Holy Spirit. Since baptism is a symbol to
show forth our identification with Christ, then
baptism is essential in order to become a part of
the visible symbol of the body of Christ on
earth, the church.

Secondly, notice that a church is made up of
those who have voluntarily united together in
organization with elected leaders and officers.
Just as one's uniting with Christ through faith is
a voluntary act on the part of the individual, so
also is his uniting with a local assembly a
voluntary act on his part. However, the local
assembly is not a loose gathering of believers
who decide to come and go at will, but an
assembled body which is organized. The
organization of the various churches or
assemblies is evidenced by the fact that different churches mentioned in the book of Acts
and the Epistles held meetings for the purpose of electing deacons, choosing representa-
tives to send to other places, selecting elders,
and disciplining some among them. The
assemblies or churches, then, are organizations
with elected leaders and officers, (Acts 6:3-7)
(Acts 14:23) (II Corinthians 8:16-24).

Thirdly, notice that a church is for the purpose of glorifying God according to the
teachings of the Bible. The only way that the

church or individual believers can glorify God is according to His Word. Therefore, it is imperative that individuals and churches diligently study the Word of God in order that they may know how to please God and glorify Him. To repeat, then, a church is a local assembly of baptized believers in one place who have voluntarily united together in organization with elected leaders and officers for the purpose of glorifying God according to the teachings of the Bible.

THE IMPORTANCE OF MEMBERSHIP IN A CHURCH

For a believer to fail to become a part of a local church is sin. Jesus Christ established the church, (Matthew 16:18); gave the qualifications and called men to be pastors of churches, (I Timothy 3:1-7) (Titus 1:5-9); and gave various gifts to some men that they could minister to the believers in the churches, (Ephesians 4:11-16). Since Christ established the church for the believers and gave gifts to men to minister to the believers in the churches, it is obvious that He intended for every believer to be a part of a local church. Since, then, the church was established for believers, not for unbelievers, the purpose of the church service is to teach the believers, build them up in the faith, and encourage them to go out and live the faith and point others to Jesus Christ for salvation. Therefore, when every service of a church is an evangelistic service, the order has been reversed and the church becomes a place for unbelievers instead of believers.

While it is true that one may be saved and assured of eternal life without belonging to a church or even without going to church, it is not possible to be a faithful and obedient christian without going to church. It is also true that one may read and study the Bible at home as a christian, but it is also true that one will not learn the Bible as well if he does not attend church, because he does not get the benefit of the gifts God has given to certain men and pastors in the church. Briefly stated, when one fails to become a part of a local church through membership, he is rebelling against the will and provision of God for him, and is therefore sinning. It is important, then, to be a member and an active part of a local church.

THE RESPONSIBILITIES OF A MEMBER TO A CHURCH

Volumes could be written on this subject by expanding upon every phase of individual responsibility to God through the church. As a member of a local church, one is to be faithful to that church because the church is the only thing on earth that Jesus Christ instituted to officially represent Him and do His work upon the earth. The faithfulness which is demanded is in several realms.

First, one should be faithful in attendance of the services of the church. Since it was established for the good of the believer, the believer is to be there in order to get the most good from it.

Secondly, one should be faithful to participate in the business meetings of the church. As believers pray and cast their votes according to the leading of the Holy Spirit, as they discern it in their lives, the will of God is made manifest to the church. One who does not exercise himself in prayer and the business of the church not only does not have any right to complain about what his church is or is not doing, but is shirking a God given responsibility and is sinning by doing so and by complaining.

Thirdly, one should be faithful in his support of the church programs. Support does not mean money only, but prayer, presence, participation, and promotion also. The church programs would include the Sunday School, the regular services, the mission program, the training programs, the special services and outreaches of the church, and any other phase of the work the church may choose to employ.

Fourthly, one should be faithful to the pastor and other elected leaders of the church. The pastor is called of God, ordained by God and men, and placed in his position by a call of God and the church congregation which verified the call of God. Therefore, since God calls a man to the position of pastor and gives to him the gifts of a pastor, then it is obvious that our Lord intends for men to submit themselves to their pastor as their leader or shepherd. The writer of the epistle to the Hebrews said, "Obey them (your leaders or guides) that have the rule over you (or guide you), and submit yourselves: for they watch for your souls, as they that must give account, that they may do it with joy, and not with grief: for that is unprofitable for you," (Hebrews 13:17).

Being faithful to the pastor does not mean that one cannot question the pastor, but it does mean that one should not publicly voice his differences with the pastor. When one has some reason to differ with his pastor, he should go to the pastor and discuss the matter in question. Most of the time the difference will be settled, or the supposed difference will be clarified by a private, open minded, Spirit directed discussion. When matters are not agreed upon after such discussion, it should be a matter of private prayer instead of public discussion, because publicly voicing such differences or discussing the differences with others privately only tends to cause strife, contention, and division, and brings shame to the church and the cause of Christ.

Fifthly, one has the responsibility of being faithful to the Lord Who is the head of the church, because one's individual behaviour outside of the church is a reflection upon the church in which he has membership. The basic responsibilities of every believer will be discussed in the next chapter.

CHAPTER IV

WHAT ONE SHOULD KNOW ABOUT CHRISTIAN LIVING

CHAPTER IV

WHAT ONE SHOULD KNOW ABOUT CHRISTIAN LIVING

There are many things involved in living a successful christian life. Many things are required of a christian in order to be faithful to the Lord and steadfast in the faith, but there are only a few simple principles that one must follow in order to live a successful christian life. When one is faithful in these five simple things, the other things required of him seem to automatically fall into place. These five things are so simple that anyone can do them, and failure to employ them in one's life as a christian guarantees failure at living a victorious and fruitful christian life. These five things are the topics for discussion in this chapter.

THE IMPORTANCE OF READING AND STUDYING THE BIBLE

The most important thing in any christian's life should be his Bible. A knowledge of the Word of God is a must. The Scriptures should take first place in any believer's life. Some may object to this by saying that they have always heard that prayer is the key to everything in the christian life. No, one does not know what prayer is, apart from the Bible. One does not know that he can pray, apart from the Bible. One does not know how to pray, apart from the Bible. One does not know who to pray to, apart from the Bible. One does not know what to pray for, apart from the Bible. One knows nothing about prayer, apart from the Bible. The Bible should take first place in the life of a saved person. Someone may object by saying that they have always heard that soul winning was the most important thing for a christian to do. No, one does not know what it means to win a soul to Christ, apart from the Bible. One does not know how to win a soul, that he can win a soul, or anything else about soul winning, apart from the Bible. The Bible must take first place in the life of a believer. One cannot minimize the importance of prayer or soul winning, but it must be recognized that the Bible is of the utmost importance to a believer. Nothing should supersede its value in the mind of a christian.

First, reading and studying the Word of God is important to a believer in order that he may grow in his spiritual life. Peter wrote, "Wherefore laying aside all malice, and all guile, and hypocrisies, and envies, and all evil speakings, As newborn babes, desire the sincere milk of the word, that ye may grow thereby: If so be ye have tasted that the Lord is gracious," (I Peter 2:1-3). Therefore, if one has been a partaker of the grace of God in salvation, he is to lay aside all bad language and habits of the old life and delight in and desire the simpler things of the Word of God, which are called milk, in order that he may grow as a christian. Just as a newborn baby must have milk, which is easy to digest, in order to grow and develop, so the individual who has partaken of the rebirth of the Holy Spirit into him must have the things from the Bible which are easily understood and digested in order to grow spiritually.

Secondly, reading and studying the Bible is

important to a believer in order that he may come to maturity in his spiritual life. The writer of the epistle to the Hebrews said,

For when for the time ye ought to be teachers, ye have need that one teach you again which be the first principles of the oracles of God; and are become such as have need of milk, and not of strong meat. For every one that useth milk is unskilful in the word of righteousness: for he is a babe. But strong meat belongeth to them that are of full age, even those who by reason of use have their senses exercised to discern both good and evil, (Hebrews 5:12-14).

What the writer of the epistle was saying was, that the Hebrew believers had been saved long enough that they should be mature enough to teach others, but they had failed to read and study, and; therefore, were still babes in Christ and had a need for milk or the very basic teachings of the Word of God themselves. He was also telling them that they were unskillful in using the Word of God, the Bible, because they were still babes in Christ as a result of not studying the Scriptures. However, he was pointing out to them in verse fourteen, that strong meat, or the things of the Bible which are difficult to understand, belongs to those who are of full age or mature in Christ, and that they are the ones who have exercised themselves in the Word of God. Therefore, if one is to mature spiritually, he is to take the milk of the Word till he develops to the point of being able to masticate and digest the meat of the Word.

In the third place, it is important for a believer to read and study the Bible in order that he may be able to work for and serve his

Lord without shame. Paul wrote to Timothy, "Study to shew thyself approved unto God, a workman that needeth not to be ashamed, rightly dividing the word of truth," (II Timothy 2:15). Notice that one is to study or give all diligence in study of the Bible in order that he might be a workman that is approved by God. Notice further that a workman for the Lord has God's approval when he is able to rightly divide or give the right interpretation or understanding of the Word of Truth or the Bible to others. In order to do that, one must spend much time reading and studying the Bible. When one fails to so study, his shame is not only before God, but before men who ask him of the hope that is within him, because he cannot give them a Scriptural answer. Peter said, "But sanctify the Lord God in your hearts: and be ready always to give an answer to every man that asketh you a reason of the hope that is in you with meekness and fear," (I Peter 3:15).

Therefore, we see that the Bible should have a very prominent place in every believer's life. It should be read and studied diligently. To fail to read and study the Bible would be to disobey God's command, and; therefore, sin.

Since the Bible is the Word of God (I Thessalonians 2:13), to read the Bible or hear it read is the same as if God stood before you and spoke to you personally. Therefore, when you read the Bible, God is talking to you. When you have someone talk to you, you usually talk to them also. Hence, you are talking one with the other. You may also talk with God. When you read the Bible, God is talking to you. When you pray, you are talking to God. The most effective Bible study should be coupled with prayer, because through prayer, one talks with the author.

THE IMPORTANCE OF REGULAR PRAYER

One short simple verse in the New Testament reveals to us the importance of prayer: "Pray without ceasing," (I Thessalonians 5:17). If the Holy Spirit thought that prayer was important enough to have the apostle Paul tell the Thessalonian believers to "pray without ceasing," then prayer must be an important part of the christian life. To pray without ceasing does not mean that one should constantly be on his knees in prayer, or that one should be constantly consciously thinking a prayer to God, or that one should always be thinking of God, but that one should always be conscious of the presence of God regardless of where he is or what he is doing, so that God may be called upon at any time or in any situation.

Jesus expressed the same thought and emphasized the importance of prayer in the parable of the unjust judge, (Luke 18:1-8). In beginning the parable, Luke stated, "And he spake a parable unto them to this end, that men ought always to pray, and not to faint," (Luke 18:1). In the parable of the importunate friend, Jesus taught that man should be consistently persistent in prayer, (Luke 11:5-10). Being faithful in prayer would include a confession of all known sin and claiming forgiveness by faith, (I John 1:9); and then praying for all men. Paul said to Timothy,

I exhort therefore, that, first of all, supplications, prayers, intercessions, and giving of thanks, be made for all men; For kings, and for all that are in authority; that we may lead a quiet and peaceable life in all godliness and honesty. For this is good and acceptable in the

sight of God our Saviour; Who will have all men to be saved, and to come unto the knowledge of the truth, (I Timothy 2:1-4).

In order for one to have effective power or influence in prayer, there are several conditions which must be met. First, the one praying must be saved. That should be obvious. Secondly, one must not harbour known sin in his life, (I John 1:9) (Psalm 66:18) (Isaiah 59:1-3). Thirdly, one must have a forgiving spirit and attitude toward others, (Matthew 6:14-15) (Mark 11:24-26). Fourthly, one must pray unselfishly, (James 4:2-3). Fifthly, one must be living in obedience to the will of God for his life, (I John 3:22). We should not make the mistake of thinking that God will give to us whatsoever we ask just because we ask for it in the name of Jesus, or because we ask for it in faith believing that He will give it to us. It is true that we must ask in faith on the merits of Jesus, but the prerequisites must be met first. When these conditions are met, then prayer avails much. When such conditions are met and prayers are being offered and answered, then we are experiencing the truth of the statement that "the effectual fervent prayer of a righteous man availeth much," (James 5:16).

If one is faithful in Bible study and fellowship with God through prayer, his natural desire will be to fellowship with others who are in fellowship with God. That is church attendance.

THE IMPORTANCE OF CHURCH ATTENDANCE

It has already been stated in chapter three that since Christ established the church, it is obvious that He expected believers to be in

attendance of church services. One must faithfully attend the services of the local church of which he is a member if he is to be an obedient christian. There are exceptions, of course, but not many people who offer excuses for not attending have valid excuses.

The author of the epistle to the Hebrews wrote to believers, "Let us hold fast the profession of our faith without wavering; (for he is faithful that promised;) And let us consider one another to provoke unto love and to good works: Not forsaking the assembling of ourselves together, as the manner of some is; but exhorting one another: and so much the more, as ye see the day approaching," (Hebrews 10:23-25). **Take particular note of a few things that are stated. First,** believers are to be considerate one of another and do things which will cause other believers to love and do good works. **Secondly,** the specific thing mentioned which christians are to do in order to provoke other believers to love and good works, is to be faithful in church attendance. Christians are told not to forsake the assembling of themselves together, which some have a habit of doing. **Thirdly,** the believers are told to exhort or encourage one another as they assemble together, and to do it even more as time passes on. The nearer we get to the second coming of Christ, the more wicked the world becomes. The more wicked the world becomes, the more difficult it becomes for a christian to keep courage and live the christian life in the world. The more difficult it becomes for christians to live in the world, the more need there is for christians to get together and exhort or encourage one another. However, what seems to be happening is the opposite to what we are told to do. As we get closer to the coming of Christ, christians are assembling together fewer times per week, and for shorter periods of time when they do meet. It is a little wonder, then, that churches are becoming weaker and believers are becoming fewer.

When christians begin to be faithful in Bible study, prayer, and church attendance, then their witness will become effective and others of the world will be brought to Christ in salvation.

THE IMPORTANCE OF WITNESSING

Jesus said, "Ye shall be witnesses unto me," (Acts 1:8). Peter said, "We are his witnesses of these things," (Acts 5:32). Paul said,

And all things are of God, who hath reconciled us to himself by Jesus Christ, and hath given to us the ministry of reconciliation; To wit, that God was in Christ, reconciling the world unto himself, not imputing their trespasses unto them; and hath committed unto us the word of reconciliation. Now then we are ambassadors for Christ, as though God did beseech you by us. we pray you in Christ's stead, be ye reconciled to God, (II Corinthians 5:18-20).

In stating that God "hath given to us the ministry of reconciliation," Paul was saying that God has given the believers a work or a job to do, and that work is that of reconciling men to God by telling them of the person and work of Jesus Christ. However, in giving that responsibility to believers, he also states that God "hath committed unto us the word of reconciliation." The "word" of reconciliation is the Bible. God has not only committed unto us a work to do, but also a Word with which to do the work.

Let us suppose that a young man marries his sweetheart, and they have a close loving relationship and fellowship. She is always honest with him, and he learns that she always means what she says and that she always does what she says she will do. One day he sins against her. In heartbroken disgust and anger, she tells him to leave, that she never wants to see him again, and that if he ever shows his face again, she will shoot him. Knowing that she has always kept her word, he leaves home with a broken heart and fear. After a few months she becomes very lonely, and decides that she was too hasty in ordering him to leave. In visiting with another young couple, she expresses her loneliness and states that she would forgive him and take him back if he would only come back to her. A few days later, the young couple are shopping in a neighboring town, and meet the young man on the street. With delight they tell him what his wife said. With skepticism he declares that he is not about to go back, because she said she would shoot him if he ever came back, and he believed what she said. They could not convince him, but did get his address. In bewilderment, they return to his wife and tell her the story. Immediately, she picks up paper and pen, writes him a letter, signs it, puts it into an envelope, and writes his name on the front of the envelope. Handing it to her friends, she asks them to take it to him. Being eager to help, her friends make a special trip to the young man's home in order to deliver the message. With trembling hands he takes the envelope and looks at his name on the front. Recognizing her handwriting, he opens the letter, reads her message of love, and believes her. Desiring her love, he returns to their home and they are reconciled.

The other young couple that was concerned and trying to help, not only had a job to do, but had a love letter with which to do it, which had the young wife's signature on it. Just so, we as believers have a work to do, but we also have a Word with which to do it, a love letter from God, and His signature is all through it. "Now then we are ambassadors for Christ."

When mankind was in the garden of Eden, he had a loving relationship and fellowship with God. One day, man sinned against God and was thereby separated from God. God has made provisions for man's reconciliation to Himself through Jesus Christ, and has given to believers the responsibility of making it known to other men. When the Word of God is delivered to men, and they recognize it as God's Word, and then believe it, they are immediately reconciled to God, or brought back into a loving relationship and fellowship with Him.

Before closing this section, we must point out what one other Bible writer has to say about the importance of witnessing. John teaches that if one is not witnessing and endeavouring to get the message of reconciliation to lost men, that he is not in fellowship with Christ, (I John 1:1-10). This does not mean that one is not saved if he fails to witness, but that he is out of fellowship. To have fellowship means to have a joint-participation in a common interest and in a common activity. To have fellowship with Christ, then, means that one must be jointly participating with Christ in a common interest and activity. The main point of interest which Christ has, is the salvation of mankind. The reason God sent His Son to the earth was to save the world, (John 3:16). The reason Jesus came to the earth was to save lost mankind, (Luke 19:10). Therefore, if anyone is to jointly participate with Christ in the interest and activity which He has, he must be witnessing to others in order that they may be saved or reconciled to God.

Witnessing, then, is a very important part of christian living. However, witnessing can be very ineffective if it is not backed by Bible study, prayer, and faithful church attendance. When one becomes genuinely interested in the salvation of others, he not only becomes faithful in the things mentioned above, but also becomes generous in his financial support of the church and the cause of Christ.

THE IMPORTANCE OF TITHING AND GIVING

The silver is mine, and the gold is mine, saith the Lord of hosts, (Haggai 2:8).

But thou shalt remember the Lord thy God: for it is he that giveth thee power to get wealth, that he may establish his covenant which he sware unto thy fathers, as it is this day, (Deuteronomy 8:18).

A close observation of the religious world will reveal that the subject of tithing and giving is ignored by some, distorted by others, abused by many, and used as a means of exploiting unsuspecting and well-meaning christians by a few who are unscrupulous. Therefore, it would behoove every christian to give some attention to the subject as it is taught in the Word of God. Such an examination will involve six different persons as they are involved with the subject.

The first person related to the subject was Abraham, (Genesis 14:17-24). Notice in verse twenty, that Abraham gave Melchizedek "tithes of all." That was the first mention of tithing to be found in the Bible. It must be noticed and remembered that tithing began with Abraham giving one-tenth of all to Melchizedek, who was the king of Salem, and "the priest of the most high God."

The second person related to the subject was Jacob, (Genesis 28:10-22). After Jacob had received the blessing from his father Isaac, and his brother Esau had threatened to kill him, his mother sent him to her brother's house in Haran. The journey required lodging at night, so he lay upon the ground and used a stone for a pillow. While he was sleeping, he dreamed a dream in which God confirmed the same covenant with him that He had made with his fathers, Isaac and Abraham. In recognition and appreciation of the promise made to him, Jacob made a vow to God, in which he said, "Of all that thou shalt give me I will surely give the tenth unto thee," (Genesis 28:22).

We see, then, that, so far as the Scriptural record is concerned, tithing began with Abraham and was continued by Jacob.

The third person related to the subject was Moses. It was through Moses that God gave the law to Israel, in which He commanded the people to tithe.

And all the tithe of the land, whether of the seed of the land, or of the fruit of the tree, is the Lord's: it is holy unto the Lord. And if a man will at all redeem ought of his tithes, he shall add thereto the fifth part thereof. And concerning the tithe of the herd, or of the flock, even of whatsoever passeth under the rod, the tenth shall be holy unto the Lord. He shall not search whether it be good or bad, neither shall he change it: and if he change it at all, then both it and the change thereof shall be holy; it shall not be redeemed. These are the commandments, which the Lord commanded Moses for the children of Israel in mount Sinai, (Leviticus 27:30-34).

Since tithing was already in practice before the law, when God commanded it in the law, He was not establishing a new thing, but simply verifying the propriety of the practice as a means of supporting His work and the priesthood, (Numbers 18:20-32). God also revealed through Moses that if anyone lived too far from the house of God, he could sell his tithe of goods, and take the tithe to the appointed place once every three years, (Deuteronomy 14:22-29). The law, then, was not the beginning of tithing, but the confirmation of tithing.

The fourth person related to the subject was Malachi. Through Malachi, the Lord said to Israel,

Even from the days of your fathers ye are gone away from mine ordinances, and have not kept them. Return unto me, and I will return unto you, saith the Lord of hosts. But ye said, Wherein shall we return? Will a man rob God? Yet ye have robbed me. But ye say, Wherein have we robbed thee? In tithes and offerings. Ye are cursed with a curse: for ye have robbed me, even this whole nation. Bring ye all the tithes into the storehouse, that there may be meat in mine house, and prove me now herewith, saith the Lord of hosts, if I will not open you the windows of heaven, and pour you out a blessing, that there shall not be room enough to receive it. And I will rebuke the devourer for your sakes, and he shall not

95

destroy the fruits of your ground; neither shall your vine cast her fruit before the time in the field, saith the Lord of hosts. And all nations shall call you blessed: for ye shall be a delight-some land, saith the Lord of hosts, (Malachi 3: 7-12).

It may be readily seen that through Malachi, tithing is commanded as a condition of receiving blessings from the Lord.

The fifth person related to the subject was Jesus. Tithing was commended by Jesus, when He said, "Woe unto you, scribes and Pharisees, hypocrites! for ye pay tithe of mint and anise and cummin, and have omitted the weightier matters of the law, judgment, mercy, and faith: these ought ye to have done, and not to leave the other undone," (Matthew 23:23). The Pharisees to whom Jesus was talking were told that tithing was right and should be practiced. Many people have objected to this portion of Scripture being used as a proof for the validity of tithing during the age of grace, because they feel that Jesus was living under the dispensation of the law at the time He spoke those words. However, Jesus also said, "The law and the prophets were until John," (Luke 16:16). If the law was until John the Baptist, then the words of Jesus concerning tithing were not spoken under the law, because John had been dead for some time before Jesus spoke on the subject. Nevertheless, for the sake of argument we shall not press the point and give the benefit of doubt to those who feel that His statement was made under the law.

The sixth person who was related to the subject was the Apostle Paul. His relationship to the subject was two-fold. First, it was through his writings that the principle of tithing was definitely revealed as a New Testament concept. Assuming that Paul wrote the book of Hebrews, notice carefully what he said.

Whither the forerunner is for us entered, even Jesus, made an high priest for ever after the order of Melchisedec. For this Melchisedec, king of Salem, priest of the most high God, who met Abraham returning from the slaughter of the kings, and blessed him; To whom also Abraham gave a tenth part of all; first being by interpretation King of righteousness, and after that also King of Salem, which is, King of peace; Without father, without mother, without descent, having neither beginning of days, nor end of life; but made like unto the Son of God; abideth a priest continually. Now consider how great this man was, unto whom even the patriarch Abraham gave the tenth of the spoils. And verily they that are of the sons of Levi, who receive the office of the priesthood, have a commandment to take tithes of the people according to the law, that is, of their brethren, though they come out of the loins of Abraham: But he whose descent is not counted from them received tithes of Abraham, and blessed him that had the promises. And without all contradiction the less is blessed of the better. And here men that die receive tithes; but there he receiveth them, of whom it is witnessed that he liveth. And as I may so say, Levi also, who receiveth tithes, payed tithes in Abraham. For he was yet in the loins of his father, when Melchisedec met him, (Hebrews 6:20-7:10).

The most prevalent objection raised against tithing is that it is a concept of the law, and christians are not under the law but under grace. However, we have already seen that

tithing began with Abraham, and was continued by Jacob, many years before the law
was given to Moses. In fact, tithing was
practiced for more than four hundred years
before the law, (Galatians 3:16-18). In the
portion of Scripture just quoted from Hebrews,
we see that Jesus was "made an high priest for
ever after the order of Melchisedec." The
priesthood man was under during the
dispensation of the law was the Levitical or
Aaronic priesthood. The priesthood man was
under before the law, when tithing began, was
the priesthood of Melchisedec. The priesthood
man is under in the dispensation of grace is the
Melchisedecan priesthood, and Jesus is the
high priest. Therefore, during this age of grace,
man is under the same priesthood he was under
when tithing began some four hundreds years
before the law. It should be clear, then, that
tithing was not a concept peculiar to the
dispensation of law, but to the age of grace, and
was only commanded under the law because it
was good and right.

It was also through the writings of Paul that it
was indicated that the tithe should be taken to
the church. When Paul went to Macedonia, he
left Timothy in charge of the church at
Ephesus, (I Timothy 1:3). After being away for
some time, Paul wrote to Timothy, and said,
"These things write I unto thee, hoping to come
unto thee shortly: But if I tarry long, that thou
mayest know how thou oughtest to behave
thyself in the house of God, which is the church
of the living God, the pillar and ground of the
truth," (I Timothy 3:14-15). In making his
statement to Timothy, Paul used a word in an
unusual manner. He used the word "church" in
reference to the building or "house." The
phrase "house of God", may be equated with

the phrase "mine house" found in Malachi 3:10. Since the tithe of the Old Testament was to be taken to the "house" of God, so the tithe of the New Testament is to be taken to the "house" of God. This position is further strengthened when we remember that the only thing our Lord instituted or established on the earth was His church or local churches. The only way, then, that one has of giving the tithe to the Lord, is through the local church just as it was given through the temple under the law.

The tithe is the Lord's, and we have no right to give it to anyone else, because it is not ours to give. If a man owes his wealthy neighbour fifty dollars, he has no right to give the fifty dollars to poor people in the community or to some good cause instead of the neighbour to whom he owes it, because it is not his to give. It belongs to the wealthy neighbour. Just so, a christian has no right to give the Lord's tithe to poor people, needy friends, preachers, or other good religious causes, because it is not his to give. It belongs to the Lord, and the only official representative He has on the earth is the churches.

A tithe is ten percent of the gross income of a wage earner, but ten percent of all increase or profit which the self employed may realize. However, a christian is expected to exceed the tithe by giving gifts and offerings. One has not made an offering or given a gift till he has already given the tithe and then given more. Gifts and offerings may be given to the Lord through the church, or one may give a gift or offering to other christian causes with which he feels the Lord would be pleased. What one personally gives to the poor, after he has given the tithe to the church, is alms giving.

To live a successful christian life, one must be

faithful in Bible study, prayer, church attendance, witnessing, and tithing and giving. These things are so simple, almost anyone can do them. Anyone who can read, can read the Bible. Anyone who can think, can pray. Anyone who is able bodied, can go to church. Anyone who can talk, can witness. Anyone who is willing, can tithe and give. These things are extremely simple but extremely important. When one is faithful in these simple things, he will find that all other things will begin to automatically fall into place in his christian life.

CHAPTER V
WHAT ONE SHOULD KNOW ABOUT PROPHECY

CHAPTER V

WHAT ONE SHOULD KNOW ABOUT PROPHECY

At this point it seems necessary to remind the reader of the purpose of this book. It is to present what I consider to be the least that every christian should be taught within a short period of time after he is saved. One may notice that the four previous chapters have been rather thorough, and that the present chapter is only a broad outline, and wonder why or perhaps be a little disappointed. While it is desirable for one to know as much about prophecy as possible, I do not feel that a knowledge of the details of Bible prophecy is as necessary to christian living as the other topics treated in this book. As one develops in his christian life and understanding; however, he should come to a fuller knowledge concerning the details of prophecy.

Bible prophecy is an intriguing subject to most people. While there are many things in prophecy that can be clearly understood, there are other prophecies that are difficult to understand. Therefore, a basic outline of the chronological order of events in prophecy can be set forth with a great degree of certainty, but one must be charitable toward differing views concerning the details of prophecy and the chronological order of some events within the details. A basic outline giving the chronological order of prophetic events will be presented in this chapter under five headings.

THE PRESENT AGE

Jesus commissioned the church to spread the gospel to all the world in this age that a people might be gathered out for Himself, (Matthew 28:18-20) (Acts 15:13-17). Although the gospel is to be preached to all nations, only a few will receive the good news, (Matthew 13:3-8). According to Paul's second letter to Timothy, this age is to end with conditions being difficult for christians to live under, and very little concern for the things of God.

This know also, that in the last days perilous times shall come. For men shall be lovers of their own selves, covetous, boasters, proud, blasphemers, disobedient to parents, unthankful, unholy, Without natural affection, trucebreakers, false accusers, incontinent, fierce, despisers of those that are good, Traitors, heady, highminded, lovers of pleasures more than lovers of God; Having a form of godliness, but denying the power thereof: from such turn away, (II Timothy 3: 1-5).

Because man will have little concern for the things of God, but still have "a form of godliness," he will evidently have a religious system which pleases him. This was implied in the words of Paul to Timothy, when he said, "for the time will come when they will not endure sound doctrine; but after their own lusts shall they heap to themselves teachers, having itching ears; And they shall turn away their ears from the truth, and shall be turned unto fables," (II Timothy 4:3-4).

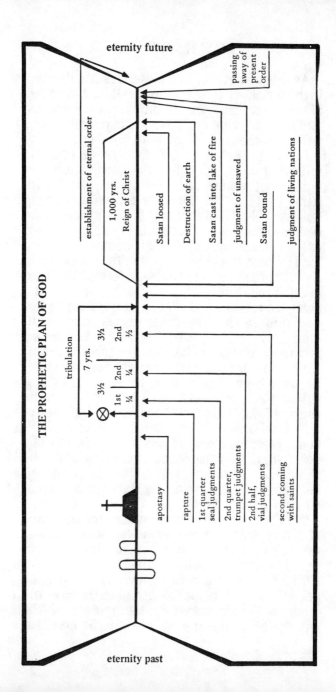

THE PROPHETIC PLAN OF GOD

eternity future

eternity past

passing away of present order

establishment of eternal order

1,000 yrs. Reign of Christ

Satan loosed

Destruction of earth

Satan cast into lake of fire

judgment of unsaved

Satan bound

judgment of living nations

tribulation

7 yrs.

3½ 2nd ½

3½ 2nd ¼

1st ¼

apostasy

rapture

1st quarter seal judgments

2nd quarter, trumpet judgments

2nd half, vial judgments

second coming with saints

THE RAPTURE

As this age comes to a close, Jesus will come in the air above the earth and call for the bodies of the dead christians to come from the graves, and for the living christians to come forth, and will take them all to be with Himself.

From I Thessalonians 4:13-18, notice the following facts. (1) When the Lord returns He will bring the souls and spirits of the saved with Him, (v:14). (2) When He comes, the living believers will not "prevent" or precede the bodies of the dead believers in going up, (v:15). (3) When He comes, He will shout a command for His own to come forth, (v:16a). (4) When He gives the command to come forth, "the dead in Christ shall rise first," (v:16b). (5) After the dead are resurrected, "Then we which are alive and remain shall be caught up together with them in the clouds, to meet the Lord in the air: and so shall we ever be with the Lord," (v:17)

A few other facts concerning the rapture may be noted from I Corinthians 15:51-53. (1) There will be some believers living on earth when the rapture takes place, (v:51a). (2) The bodies of all christians will be changed to a glorified body, whether living or dead, (v:51b). (3) The dead shall be raised and the living shall be changed instantly, (v:52). (4) All raptured believers will receive a new body which cannot corrupt or die, (v:53).

There are several views concerning the place of the rapture in time. Some teach that it will take place after the tribulation, others affirm that it will happen in the middle of the tribulation, still others believe that it will be split with faithful believers taken before and other believers taken in the middle of the tribulation, and some believe it to be an event that will take place before the tribulation begins. Most premillennialists teach that it will take place before the tribulation. That it will take place before the tribulation appears to be the Scriptural viewpoint. However, there are different viewpoints among the pre-tribulation rapturists. Some believe that it may take place at any moment. Others teach that there are other prophecies to be fulfilled before the rapture can take place. However, both schools of thought agree that this age will end with the apostasy and the revelation of the Antichrist, and then the rapture will take place which will be the beginning of the tribulation.

THE TRIBULATION

The tribulation will begin after the rapture and will last for a period of seven years, (Daniel 9:24-27). The term "tribulation" refers to the total seven years period in which God's wrath will be poured out upon the earth, which will basically be a purging of the Jews in order to make them recognize and acknowledge that Jesus Christ was actually the Messiah that God had promised to them. The term "abomination of desolation" refers to the great abomination that will take place in Israel at the middle point of the tribulation. The Antichrist will make a covenant with Israel for seven years, but after three and one half years he will break the covenant and declare himself to be God. The term "great tribulation" refers to the second half of the tribulation when God's wrath will be more severe and when the persecution of Jews will be intensified by the Antichrist. It must be kept in mind also that "tribulation" refers to what God pours out upon mankind on the earth, and that "persecution" refers to what man does to man.

The chronological order of events during the tribulation as they will be on earth are recorded in Revelation, chapters six, eight, nine, and sixteen. The seal judgments which are recorded in chapter six, take place during the first quarter of the tribulation in the order recorded. The trumpet judgments which are recorded in chapters eight and nine, take place during the second quarter of the tribulation in the order recorded. The vial or bowl judgments which are recorded in chapter sixteen, take place during the second half of the tribulation in the order recorded. Although the judgments begin during the periods of the tribulation mentioned above, they are not confined to that given portion of the tribulation for duration. Some of the judgments last for a period of time long enough for several judgments to be in progress at one time.

The judgments and the wars of the tribulation will be so severe, and the lives of so many men will be taken, that by the end of the seven year period, there will be seven women for each man, (Isaiah 4:1).

As the tribulation comes to a close, Israel will acknowledge her national sin of rejection, recognize Jesus Christ as her Messiah, and will pray for His return. At that point, Jesus shall return to the earth.

For I will be unto Ephraim as a lion, and as a young lion to the house of Judah: I, even I, will tear and go away; I will take away, and none shall rescue him. I will go and return to my place, till they acknowledge their offence, and seek my face: in their affliction they will seek me early. Come, and let us return unto the Lord: for he hath torn, and he will heal us; he hath smitten, and he will bind us up. After two days will he revive us: in the third day he will raise us up, and we shall live in his sight. Then shall we know, if we follow on to know the Lord: his going forth is prepared as the morning; and he shall come unto us as the rain, as the latter and former rain unto the earth, (Hosea 5:14-6:3).

THE SECOND COMING

The second coming is a phrase that is many times used to refer to the rapture and the return of Christ to the earth. It is stated that the second coming is in two phases; the rapture which takes place before the tribulation, and the revelation of Christ which takes place after the tribulation. It seems more literal and less confusing to refer to the coming of Christ in the air to take the saints to be with Him, as the rapture. At the time of the rapture, He does not come to the earth, therefore, it is not a second coming. When He came the first time, He came to the earth. When He comes the second time, He will come to the earth again. Just so, it is also a more literal usage to refer to His coming to the earth at the end of the tribulation as the second coming, because that is the time at which He will actually come to the earth the second time. It must be realized, however, that the two schools of thinking are identical in position. It is only the usage of the terms that are different.

After Jesus has returned to the earth at the end of the tribulation and subdued the forces of evil, the judgment of the living nations of people will take place, (Matthew 25:31-46). He will set up a one world government and rule as king of the earth from the throne of David, in Jerusalem. We, the saints who have returned with Him, will rule and reign with Him for a thousand years, (Isaiah 9:6-7) (Jeremiah 3:17; 23:5-6) (Zephaniah 3:15) (Zechariah 14:9).

The conditions which will prevail during the reign of Christ are fascinating. First, there will be perfect justice, (Isaiah 11:3-5). The justice will be perfect because Jesus will be the judge. He will have no need of a jury or of witnesses. Because He is God, He will perfectly understand each case and judge according to His perfect knowledge and righteousness.

Secondly, there will be a complete possession of the promised land by the Israelites, (Jeremiah 3:18; 16:14-15) (Obadiah 17). God promised the land to Abraham and his seed in an unconditional promise. Therefore, there must be a time when Israel will possess the whole land. To this point in history they have never possessed it, but will during the reign of Christ.

Thirdly, there will be no wars during the time that Christ reigns as king of the earth, (Isaiah 2:4) (Micah 4:3). Not only will there be no wars, but there will be no instruments of war because they will all be made into instruments of peace.

Fourthly, there will be streams of water in the deserts, and Israel and the world will enjoy a time of agricultural prosperity, (Isaiah 35:1-7) (Ezekiel 36:33-35) (Joel 2:21-24).

Fifthly, there will be no carnivorous animals, (Isaiah 11:6-9) (Isaiah 65:25). Some teachers explain this as the condition that will exist in heaven. However, it must be noted that the word "earth" is used. The reason that there will be no hurting nor destroying will be because of the full knowledge of the Lord that all will have at that time.

In the sixth place, there will be no false religions, but a worship of the Lord only, (Zechariah 8:20-23) (Micah 5:10-15). This does not mean that all people will be saved and worship the Lord, but that there will be no other worship permitted other than the worship of the Lord.

In the seventh place, there will be a perfect knowledge of the Lord during His reign, (Isaiah 11:9; 35:8). Although everyone will have a perfect understanding about the Lord, everyone will not accept Him for salvation.

In the eight place, there will be a common language, (Zephaniah 3:9). The work of God in confounding the languages at Babel, (Genesis 11:7), will be reversed for the millennium.

In the ninth place, there will be no hinderance from Satan during the thousand years that Christ will reign as king, because he will be bound during that period of time, (Revelation 20:1-3). Think of it. Today we are tempted by the world, the flesh, and the Devil. During the reign of Christ, man will be tempted only by his sinful flesh, because the Devil will be bound, the world will be restored to purity, and all will have a full knowledge of the Lord. Even under those conditions, we are told that the majority of men will reject Christ for their salvation. Certainly, our sinful flesh is our greatest enemy.

Last of all, there will be a restoration of long life as there was before the flood, (Isaiah 65:20). Supposedly, this will be true because the atmospheric conditions that prevailed before the flood, will exist again during the millennium.

When the reign of Christ comes to an end on

earth, He delivers up the kingdom to the Father "that God may be all in all," (I Corinthians 15:20-28).

THE END

At the end of the reign of Christ, Satan will be loosed from his prison, will go out into the earth and gather those who are unbelievers to make up an army, and will make an attack on Jerusalem in a last effort to defeat Jesus Christ. As they approach Jerusalem, fire will come down from heaven to destroy them. After they are destroyed, the Devil will be cast into the eternal lake of fire; the unsaved will be resurrected and brought before the great white throne to be judged, and they all will be cast into the eternal lake of fire which is the second death; and the existing heaven and earth will pass away into nothingness, (Revelation 20:7-15).

The saints who will reign upon the earth with Christ, and the people who will be saved during His reign, will all be delivered from the fire that will fall upon the earth to destroy it, and will live upon a new perfect earth with Christ in peaceful bliss forever.

And I saw a new heaven and a new earth: for the first heaven and the first earth were passed away; and there was no more sea. And I John saw the holy city, new Jerusalem, coming down from God out of heaven, prepared as a bride adorned for her husband. And I heard a great voice out of heaven saying, Behold, the tabernacle of God is with men, and he will dwell with them, and they shall be his people, and God himself shall be with them, and be their God. And God shall wipe away all tears from their eyes; and there shall be no more death, neither sorrow, nor crying, neither shall there be any more pain: for the former things are passed away. And he that sat upon the throne said, Behold, I make all things new. And he said unto me, Write: for these words are true and faithful. And he said unto me, It is done. I am Alpha and Omega, the beginning and the end. I will give unto him that is athirst of the fountain of the water of life freely. He that overcometh shall inherit all things; and I will be his God, and he shall be my son, (Revelation 21:1-7).

APPENDIX A
THE DEATH OF CHRIST

APPENDIX A

THE DEATH OF CHRIST

In the New Testament, the death of Jesus Christ is defined several ways, but all point to the same truth that He died in order to save man from the condemnation of sin which is the eternal lake of fire. The word "salvation" is a term which has many sub-topics. To save carries the meaning of salvaging, to save for original purpose. Man was created by God, and therefore belonged to God, for the purpose of fellowshiping with God and glorifying Him. When man sinned in Adam, he became separated from God, sold under sin, and became the possession of Satan. As such, man could no longer fellowship with God or glorify Him. Therefore, when God saves a man, He is salvaging him for the purpose of glorifying Him and fellowshiping with Him. While in this present body of flesh, though saved, man can fellowship with God and glorify Him, but not to the extent that he did before Adam sinned, and not to the extent he will be able to after the body is also saved. The price which God paid in order to buy man back into His possession in order that He might salvage man for his original purpose, was that of His only begotten Son, Jesus Christ. In speaking of the death of His Son, the New Testament expresses four different ideas, but all four pointing to the same end, the salvation of man.

First, the death of Jesus Christ is defined as a

ransom or a redemption. A ransom is a price paid to buy back, and a redemption is the transaction which takes place in buying back. During His earthly ministry, Jesus declared that His purpose in coming to the earth was to give His own life as the ransom price for the many of mankind. "Even as the Son of man came not to be ministered unto, but to minister, and to give his life a ransom (the price paid to buy back) for many," (Matthew 20:28). After Christ had accomplished His purpose, Paul wrote to those in Galatia who had been saved and said, "Christ hath redeemed (bought back) us from the curse of the law, being made a curse for us: for it is written, Cursed is every one that hangeth on a tree," (Galatians 3:13). By hanging on a tree or a cross, Jesus died in order to buy man back from the condemnation. From the statement which Paul made to the young preacher Timothy, we learn that the ransom price paid by Jesus was for all men without exception. "For there is one God, and one mediator between God and men, the man Christ Jesus; Who gave himself a ransom (the price paid to buy back) for all, to be testified in due time," (I Timothy 2:5-6). Peter, in writing to fellow believers reminded them that they had not been redeemed or bought back by anything but the blood of Christ which was shed for them.

Forasmuch as ye know that ye were not redeemed with corruptible things, as silver and gold, from your vain conversation received by tradition from your fathers; But with the precious blood of Christ, as of a lamb without blemish and without spot: Who verily was foreordained before the foundation of the world, but was manifest in these last times for you, (I Peter 1:18-20).

In the revelation which John received from Jesus, he recorded a scene that is yet to take place in heaven when the saved will give honour and praise to Jesus for redeeming (buying back) them to God by His blood. "And they sung a new song, saying, Thou art worthy to take the book, and to open the seals thereof: for thou wast slain, and hast redeemed us (bought us back) to God by thy blood out of every kindred, and tongue, and people, and nation," (Revelation 5:9). We see then that the death of Jesus Christ was a ransom price paid in order to redeem (buy back) mankind from the ownership of Satan, the power of sin, and the condemnation, and to buy man back into God's ownership. Being thus purchased, He is our owner, our master, our Lord.

Secondly, the death of Jesus Christ is defined as a substitution. Man was the one who sold himself under sin and to Satan, and therefore was the one who was responsible for buying himself back. Man was the one who owed the debt. However, man was bankrupt and not capable of paying the price, so Christ as man's substitute paid it for him. Peter, in writing to his brethren, said concerning Jesus, "Who His own self bare our sins in His own body on the tree," (I Peter 2:24). Later, Peter said, "For Christ also hath once suffered for sins, the just for the unjust, that he might bring us to God, being put to death in the flesh, but quickened by the Spirit," (I Peter 3:18). The purpose of this substitutionary work was to take our sin upon Himself, that His righteousness might be applied to us. Paul said to the Corinthian believers, "For He (God) hath made Him (Jesus) to be sin for us, who knew no sin; that we might be made the righteousness of God in Him (Jesus)," (II Corinthians 5:21).

Thirdly, the death of Jesus Christ is defined as a propitiation. The propitiation of the New Testament is identified with the Mercy Seat of the Old Testament. The Mercy Seat was the place where amends for sin were made and the place where God's justice and wrath was satisfied on behalf of the sinner. In the New Testament, Jesus Christ is found to be not only the place where amends and satisfaction for sin is made, but also to be that which makes amends for the sin of man and satisfies the justice and wrath of God on behalf of the sinner. Writing to believers concerning Jesus Christ, John has said, "He is the propitiation (the one who makes amends) for our sins: and not for our's only, but also for the sins of the whole world," (I John 2:2). Concerning the love of God, John wrote, "Herein is love, not that we loved God, but that he loved us, and sent his Son to be the propitiation (the one who makes amends) for our sins," (I John 4:10). God sent His Son to make amends for us because we were not capable of making amends for ourselves. But, let us suppose that man did have the capability of paying the price to make amends. He still could not do so, because he is unholy and God is holy. Therefore, an unholy man could not make an approach to a holy God to make an offering that amends might be made. He must remain forever separated from God. Therefore, God in His love provided the propitiation for man.

Fourthly, the death of Jesus Christ is defined as a reconciliation. A reconciliation is a bringing back together. In the beginning, man had a close relationship and fellowship with God. After man sinned, he was separated from God and became the natural enemy of God.

However, through the death of Jesus Christ, man may be brought back into a loving relationship and fellowship with God. Paul wrote to the church in Rome, "when we were enemies, we were reconciled to God by the death of his Son," (Romans 5:10). Once we have been reconciled to God, it is our responsibility to take the message of reconciliation to others.

And all things are of God, who hath reconciled us to himself by Jesus Christ, and hath given to us the ministry of reconciliation; To wit, that God was in Christ, reconciling the world unto himself, not imputing their trespasses unto them; and hath committed unto us the word of reconciliation. Now then we are ambassadors for Christ, as though God did beseech you by us: we pray you in Christ's stead, be ye reconciled to God, (II Corinthians 5:18-20).

Notice the logical sequence of these terms. Man sold himself under sin and to Satan and was under the condemnation. Jesus Christ died upon the cross and shed His blood there in order to buy man back from the condemnation. Man was the one who owed the debt, but was not able to pay, so Christ Jesus paid it for him as a substitute. In offering Himself up to God in the place of man, the justice of God was satisfied, His wrath was appeased, and amends were made for man's sin. Jesus Christ was propitious for our sins and God was propitiated. Once the amends for sin had been made and God's wrath and justice was satisfied, man could once again go before God on the merits of what Christ Jesus had done and have a loving relationship and fellowship with God.

Since Jesus thus purchased us from the

condemnation and redeemed us to God, He
certainly is our Lord and we should not be
ashamed to admit it.

The summation of it all is given by Paul in his
letter to the Romans.

*Now we know that what things soever the law
saith, it saith to them who are under the law:
that every mouth may be stopped, and all the
world may become guilty before God.
Therefore by the deeds of the law there shall no
flesh be justified in his sight: for by the law is
the knowledge of sin. But now the righteousness
of God without the law is manifested, being
witnessed by the law and the prophets; Even
the righteousness of God which is by faith of
Jesus Christ unto all and upon all them that
believe: for there is no difference: For all have
sinned, and come short of the glory of God;
Being justified freely by his grace through the
redemption that is in Christ Jesus: Whom God
hath set forth to be a propitiation through faith
in his blood, to declare his righteousness for the
remission of sins that are past, through the
forbearance of God; To declare, I say, at this
time his righteousness: that he might be just,
and the justifier of him which believeth in
Jesus. Where is boasting then? It is excluded.
By what law? of works? Nay: but by the law of
faith. Therefore we conclude that a man is
justified by faith without the deeds of the law. Is
he the God of the Jews only? is he not also of the
Gentiles? Yes, of the Gentiles also: Seeing it is
one God, which shall justify the circumcision by
faith, and uncircumcision through faith,
(Romans 3:19-30).*

APPENDIX B
SALVATION AND ASSURANCE BY FAITH ALONE

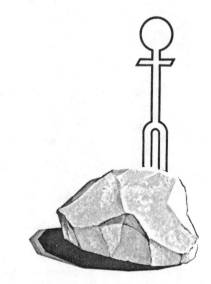

APPENDIX B

SALVATION AND ASSURANCE BY FAITH ALONE

And they journeyed from mount Hor by the way of the Red sea, to compass the land of Edom: and the soul of the people was much discouraged because of the way. And the people spake against God, and against Moses, Wherefore have ye brought us up out of Egypt to die in the wilderness? for there is no bread, neither is there any water; and our soul loatheth this light bread. And the Lord sent fiery serpents among the people, and they bit the people; and much people of Israel died. Therefore the people came to Moses, and said, We have sinned. for we have spoken against the Lord, and against thee; pray unto the Lord, that he take away the serpents from us. And Moses prayed for the people. And the Lord said unto Moses, Make thee a fiery serpent, and set it upon a pole: and it shall come to pass, that every one that is bitten, when he looketh upon it, shall live. And Moses made a serpent of brass, and put it upon a pole, and it came to pass, that if a serpent had bitten any man, when he beheld the serpent of brass, he lived, (Numbers 21:4-9).

When Jesus was talking to Nicodemus and telling him how to be saved, He made reference to that wilderness experience and said, "And as Moses lifted up the serpent in the wilderness, even so must the Son of man be lifted up: That whosoever believeth in him should not perish, but have eternal life," (John 3:14-15). In that wilderness experience, people were being bitten by poisonous snakes and were dying. The Lord told Moses to make a snake out of brass and set it up upon a pole in the camp of Israel, and to tell the people that if they would look at the brazen serpent and believe God, that He would heal them and save them from a physical death. Jesus told Nicodemus that He, the Son of God, must be lifted up upon a pole or cross, and that all who would look to Him and believe God would be saved, not from a physical death, but from the eternal second death into an eternal life. Therefore if one believes in Jesus Christ, the Son of God, he must also believe that he will never perish in the lake of fire just because he believes in Jesus. If one believes in Jesus, he must also believe that he now has eternal life just because he believes in Jesus.

In further explanation to Nicodemus, Jesus said, "For God so loved the world, that he gave his only begotten Son, that whosoever believeth in him should not perish, but have everlasting life," (John 3:16). Jesus said that God gave His Son in order to save the world of mankind from perishing in the lake of fire, and that whosoever would believe in Jesus would not perish in the eternal lake of fire but would have everlasting life. Since Jesus cannot lie, and God's Word has to be true, then whosoever believes in Jesus Christ must also have enough confidence in God's Word and promise to believe that he will not perish in hell or the lake of fire. Also, one who believes in Jesus must believe that he has everlasting life just because he believes, because God said he would have everlasting life by believing, and God cannot lie.

Before leaving Nicodemus, Jesus said, "For

God sent not his Son into the world to condemn the world; but that the world through him might be saved. He that believeth on him is not condemned: but he that believeth not is condemned already, because he hath not believed in the name of the only begotten Son of God,'' (John 3:17-18). Notice that Jesus said that anyone who believes on Him is not condemned. Therefore, anyone who believes and accepts the fact that Jesus is the Saviour He claims to be, must also believe that he is saved from the condemnation just because he believes in that Saviour, because Jesus Christ said he would be. But notice that He also said that if anyone does not believe in Him, he is condemned already just because he has not believed in Jesus as the Son of God in order to be saved from the condemnation. It is interesting to note that Jesus said nothing about sin but much about the sin bearer. Jesus Christ Himself bore our sins in His own body and paid the redemptive price to buy all men back from the condemnation, as has been explained in appendix A. Therefore, those who believe on Him or accept His sacrificial work on their behalf by faith, are saved from the condemnation, but those who refuse to believe that they are saved from the condemnation by simply believing on the person and work of Christ on their behalf, are already condemned simply because they refuse to believe the word of the omnipotent and omniscient God, which says that they would be saved if they would only trust Him.

There are many portions of scripture in the New Testament which express the same thought, that a person is saved just because he believes in Jesus and has faith to believe that he is saved just because he believes in Jesus. Several of them are quoted below and the reader is encouraged to read each one thoughtfully with a few questions in mind. As you read the following verses, ask yourself: Do I believe in Jesus? Do I have everlasting life? If so, why? If not, why not? Will I ever perish in hell and the eternal lake of fire? If not, why not? If so, why?

He that believeth on the Son hath everlasting life: and he that believeth not the Son shall not see life; but the wrath of God abideth on him, (John 3:36).

Verily, verily, I say unto you, He that heareth my word, and believeth on him that sent me, hath everlasting life, and shall not come into condemnation; but is passed from death unto life, (John 5:24).

And this is the will of him that sent me, that every one which seeth the Son, and believeth on him, may have everlasting life: and I will raise him up at the last day, (John 6:40).

Verily, verily, I say unto you, He that believeth on me hath everlasting life, (John 6:47).

I said therefore unto you, that ye shall die in your sins: for if ye believe not that I am he, ye shall die in your sins, (John 8:24).

Jesus said unto her, I am the resurrection, and the life: he that believeth in me, though he were dead, yet shall he live: And whosoever liveth and believeth in me shall never die. Believest thou this? (John 11:25-26).

I am come a light into the world, that whosoever believeth on me should not abide in darkness. And if any man hear my words, and believe not, I judge him not: for I came not to judge the world, but to save the world. He that rejecteth me, and receiveth not my words, hath one that judgeth him: the word that I have spoken, the same shall judge him in the last day, (John 12:46-48).

Jesus saith unto him, I am the way, the truth, and the life: no man cometh unto the Father, but by me, (John 14:6).

And many other signs truly did Jesus in the presence of his disciples, which are not written in this book: But these are written, that ye might believe that Jesus is the Christ, the Son of God; and that believing ye might have life through his name, (John 20:30-31).

Man must believe, put his faith in, have confidence in, depend upon, rely upon, accept, receive the fact that Jesus Christ died and shed His blood in order to buy him back from the condemnation of sin; and believe, put his faith in, have confidence in, depend upon, rely upon, accept, receive the fact that God raised Him from the dead in a body for his justification, in order to be saved. One who claims to believe these things but cannot by faith claim salvation on the basis of his faith in the promise of God, has called God a liar and said that God is not trustworthy, because God has said that he would be saved by believing.

If we receive the witness of men, the witness of God is greater: for this is the witness of God which he hath testified of his Son. He that believeth on the Son of God hath the witness in himself: he that believeth not God hath made him a liar; because he believeth not the record that God gave of his Son. And this is the record, that God hath given to us eternal life, and this life is in his Son. He that hath the Son hath life; and he that hath not the Son of God hath not life. These things have I written unto you that believe on the name of the Son of God; that ye may know that ye have eternal life, and that ye may believe on the name of the Son of God, (I John 5:9-13).

APPENDIX C

THE SCRIPTURAL USAGE OF THE WORD "CHURCH"

APPENDIX C

THE SCRIPTURAL USAGE OF THE WORD "CHURCH"

There is much controversy and many strange concepts concerning the church in this present age. This truth is evidenced by a look at the definition of the word as it appears in an English dictionary. Any standard unabridged dictionary of the English language will reveal that the word "church", carries such meanings as follows: A building in which christians meet, the religious activities carried on by an assembly of christians, a local assembly of christians, any number of local assemblies associating together because of common beliefs, the total of all christian believers, the authority of ecclesiastical bodies, the ministerial profession, any religious body, or any building in which religious bodies meet.

Many dogmatically declare that the only concept that God ever intended to convey by the word "church" is that of a local assembly of christians. Others assiduously assume that the word should always be thought of as carrying the idea of a universal intangible invisible body into which every believer is placed at the moment of his salvation. This idea implies that the church exists apart from believers, and that believers are simply placed into a body-shell to fill it as they are saved. There are many others who hold to various positions on the scale between these two positions. However, the main controversy is between the idea of a universal invisible church and the idea of a local visible church. Much has been written and even more has been said on both sides of the issue in an attempt to persuade others that one or the other position is the Biblical position. However, one cannot come to a satisfactory and rational conclusion on the subject until he has carefully defined and closely examined all references to the word in the New Testament.

THE DEFINITION OF CHURCH

We have already seen the indefinite meaning the word has come to convey in the English language, but we must establish its intended meaning by its usage in the New Testament. The Greek word that is rendered as "Church" in our English Bibles is "ekklasia." Berry renders the word as "assembly", and in his lexicon defines it as, "an assembly, usually legally, sometimes tumultuously gathered. Especially in N.T., an assembly of christian believers, a church in one place, often plural."[1] Rotherham renders the word as "assembly", and says, "It is well-known that the Greek word for 'church' is ecclesia; and that ecclesia strictly and fully means 'called-out-assembly'."[2] Wuest says, "the word 'assembly' is a good one-word translation of ekklesia."[3] Vincent says, "orginally an assembly of citizens, regularly summoned. ...

1 From *The Interlinear Greek-English New Testament* by George Ricker Berry, Copyright 1969 by Zondervan Publishing House and is used by permission.

2 Joseph Bryant Rotherham, *The Emphasized Bible*, Grand Rapids, Kregel Publications, 1971, p:268.

3 Kenneth Wuest, *Studies in the Vocabulary of the Greek New Testament*, Grand Rapids, Wm. B. Eerdmans Publishing Company, 1962, p:27.

In the New Testament the term is used also in the narrower sense of a single church, or a church confined to a particular place."[4] Bernard says, "the ekklasia in question is the local christian community over which the episkopos is placed."[5] Further, he explains, "The term ekklasia, representing the kahal of the O.T., has, like its Hebrew original, a double meaning, sometimes being used for the local christian congregation, sometimes in the larger sense of the new Israel in covenant relation with God."[6] Green, in his lexicon says, "A popular assembly; in N.T., the congregation of the children of Israel, transferred to the christian body, of which the congregation of Israel was a figure, the church; a local portion of the church, a local church; a christian congregation."[7] Harper and Brothers lexicon states, "A popular assembly; the congregation of the children of Israel, transferred to the christian body, of which the congregation of Israel was a figure, the church; a local portion of the church, a local church; a christian congregation."[8] Strong says, "calling out, a popular meeting, especially a religious congregation."[9] In determining the meaning

4 Marvin R. Vincent, *Word Studies in the New Testament*, Grand Rapids, Wm. B. Eerdmans Publishing Company, 1969, p:93.

5 J. H. Bernard, *Cambridge Greek New Testament for Schools and Colleges — The Pastoral Epistles*, Cambridge, The University Press, 1906, p:55.

6 Ibid., p:61.

7 From *A Greek-English Lexicon of the New Testament* by Thomas Sheldon Green, Copyright 1971 by Zondervan Publishing House and is used by permission.

8 *The Analytical Greek Lexicon*, New York, Harper and Brothers Publishers, n.d., pp:124-125.

9 James Strong, *The Exhaustive Concordance of the Bible*, "Greek Dictionary of the New Testament", New York, Abingdon Press, 1958, p:26.

of the word "ekklasia", it is important to notice that the emphasis is always on "assembling", but not always on the "called out." A church, then, seems to be a group of people who have been called out and assembled together in some place. However, before one can draw a final conclusion on the meaning and usage of the word, there must be a delineation of the word as it appears in context in the New Testament.

THE DELINEATION OF CHURCH

The Greek word "ekklasia" appears in the New Testament a total of one hundred and twelve times. An examination of each occurrence should shed some light on the New Testament usage of the word. These will be surveyed through the New Testament as they occur from the first to the last, and at the end of each one, one of three letters will be placed; an "L" after those referring to a local assembly, a "U" after those referring to an invisible universal assembly, and a "Q" after those concerning which there could be doubt, uncertainty, or question.

1. "Upon this rock I will build my church (assembly)," (Matthew 16:18). This is the first usage of the word in the New Testament, and there is much controversy over its intended meaning. (Q)

2,3. "And if he shall neglect to hear them, tell it unto the Church (assembly): but if he neglect to hear the church (assembly), let him be unto thee as an heathen man and a publican," (Matthew 18:17). There should be no question but what this passage of Scripture refers to a local assembly of believers, because that is the only kind of an assembly that could listen to information concerning an individual or give direction to an individual. (L)

4. "And the Lord added to the church (assembly) daily such as should be saved," (Acts 2:47). Some argue that this is speaking of additions to the universal body of Christ, while others argue that "the church" makes reference to the local church in Jerusalem. (Q)

5. "And great fear came upon all the church (assembly)," (Acts 5:11). Beyond question, this speaks of a local situation. The local assembly which saw the death of Ananias and Sapphira feared. The universal body could not have known of the incident and, therefore, could not have feared. (L)

6. "This is he, that was in the church (assembly) in the wilderness," (Acts 7:38). Although this speaks of Israel in the wilderness, they were an organized body in one place and were assembled. (L)

7. "And at that time there was a great persecution against the church (assembly) which was at (in) Jerusalem; and they were all scattered abroad throughout the regions of Judaea and Samaria, except the apostles," (Acts 8:1). This evidently speaks of the local assembly in Jerusalem which was being scattered, else Luke would have said the church in Jerusalem, Judaea, and Samaria. (L)

8. "He made havoc of the church (assembly)," (Acts 8:3). Here, the church at Jerusalem is evidently meant. Many assume that Paul persecuted many different local churches, and then apply the word "church" in Acts 8:3, and other passages to the multiplicity of churches.

There is no evidence that the word "church" is ever used in reference to "churches" as a whole, especially when used in reference to Paul's persecution of the church. The only Scriptural indication that Paul persecuted churches other than the church in Jerusalem, is found in his defense before Agrippa. "And I punished them oft in every synagogue, and compelled them to blaspheme; and being exceedingly mad against them, I persecuted them even unto strange cities," (Acts 26:11). When Paul testified that he "persecuted them even unto strange cities", he was not speaking of churches, but of individual Jews in the synagogues. Only a casual reading of the context will make this fact evident.

It seems rather clear that the local assembly at Jerusalem is in view here. However, for the sake of argument, we will give the benefit of doubt to the universal concept. (Q)

9.   "Then had the churches (assemblies) rest (peace) throughout all Judaea and Galilee and Samaria, and were edified (built up)," (Acts 9:31). The mention of the plurality of assemblies makes it evident that local churches or assemblies are meant. (L)

10. "Then tidings of these things came unto the ears of the church (assembly) which was in Jerusalem," (Acts 11:22). Only a local assembly, not a universal invisible body, could hear of people being saved in Antioch. (L)

11. "And it came to pass, that a whole year they assembled themselves with (in) the church (assembly), and taught much people," (Acts 11:26). Paul and Barnabas

assembled with the people in Antioch for one year and taught them. This could be nothing but a local assembly of people. (L)

12. "Now about that time Herod the king stretched forth his hands to vex (ill-treat) certain of the church (assembly)," (Acts 12:1). The context reveals that this took place in Jerusalem, that James was killed, and Peter was imprisoned to be killed but was delivered by the Lord. This, then, also speaks of the church or assembly in Jerusalem. (L)

13. "Peter therefore was kept in prison: but prayer was made without ceasing (earnestly) of (by) the church (assembly) unto God for him," (Acts 12:5). This verse is in the same context as the one above and, therefore, speaks of the local church or assembly in Jerusalem. (L)

14. "Now there were in the church that was at (in) Antioch certain prophets and teachers," (Acts 13:1). Only a casual reading of this portion of Scripture readily reveals that the reference is to a local church. (L)

15. "And when they had ordained (appointed by stretching forth the hand) them elders in every church (assembly), and had prayed with fasting, they commended them to the Lord," (Acts 14:23). If there was only one universal church, then elders could not be ordained in "every church." (L)

16. "And when they were come, and had gathered the church (assembly) together, they rehearsed all that God had done with them," (Acts 14:27). Paul and Barnabas "gathered the church together" in Antioch, and told them what God had done in other

places. A local church at Antioch is evidently meant. (L)

17. "And being brought on their way by the church (assembly), they passed through Phenice and Samaria," (Acts 15:3). The church at Antioch was sending Paul, Barnabas, and others to Jerusalem. (L)

18. "And when they were come to Jerusalem, they were received of (by) the church (assembly), and of the apostles and elders," (Acts 15:4). It is evident that the local church at Jerusalem is meant. (L)

19. "Then pleased it the apostles and elders, with the whole church (assembly), to send chosen men of their own company to Antioch with Paul and Barnabas," (Acts 15:22). The Church in Jerusalem sent Paul, Barnabas, and others back to Antioch with a letter to the Church in Antioch. (L)

20. "And he went through Syria and Cilicia, confirming the churches (assemblies)," (Acts 15:41). To confirm "churches", there had to be not only a universal body, but several local bodies. (L)

21. "And so were the churches (assemblies) established in the faith, and increased in number daily," (Acts 16:5). For churches to be established, there had to be more than one. Therefore, local churches are meant. (L)

22. "And when he had landed at Caesarea, and gone up, and saluted the church (assembly), he went down to Antioch," (Acts 18:22). Here we find that Paul greeted the church in Caesarea and then went on to Antioch. This, of course, speaks of a church in a given locality. (L)

23. "Some therefore cried one thing, and some another: for the assembly was confused,"

(Acts 19:32). The people who were assembled in Ephesus on this occasion were not believers, but they were assembled together in a local area. (L)

24. "But if ye enquire any thing concerning other matters, it shall be determined in a lawful assembly," (Acts 19:39). Here, the townclerk of Ephesus told the people who were assembled on that occasion that they were not to take the law into their own hands, but that matters should be decided in a lawful assembly. This assembly, of course, would be a localized assembly. (L)

25. "And when he had thus spoken, he dismissed the assembly," (Acts 19:41). It is simply stated here that the people assembled in Ephesus were dismissed. (L)

26. "And from Miletus he sent to Ephesus, and called the elders of the church (assembly)," (Acts 20:17). In this portion of Scripture we are told that Paul called for the elders of the church in Ephesus to meet him in Miletus. This obviously refers to the local church in Ephesus. (L)

27. "Feed the church (assembly) of God," (Acts 20:28). Paul admonished the Ephesian elders to feed the church or assembly over which they were overseers. It is obvious that they were not over all believers and admonished to feed them, but were over the believers in the local assembly at Ephesus and expected to feed them. (L)

28. "I commend unto you Phoebe our sister, which is a servant of the church (assembly) which is at Cenchrea," (Romans 16:1). This obviously speaks of a particular person in a particular local assembly. (L)

29. "Unto whom not only I give thanks, but

also all the churches (assemblies) of the Gentiles," (Romans 16:4). Since more than one church or assembly is spoken of, it naturally follows that local churches are meant instead of a single universal church. (L)

30. "Likewise greet the church (assembly) that is in their house," (Romans 16:5). Paul sends greetings to the church which is in the house of Priscilla and Aquila. The universal church could not possibly dwell in one house, therefore, one local church is obviously in view here. (L)

31. "The churches (assemblies) of Christ salute you," (Romans 16:16). Since the word is plural, it naturally follows that the reference must be to local assemblies. (L)

32. "Gaius mine host, and of the whole church (assembly), saluteth you," (Romans 16:23). Gaius is spoken of as the host of Paul and the whole church. Since he could not be the host of the universal body, the reference must be to the church Paul was with when writing the epistle. (L)

33. "Unto the church (assembly) of God which is at Corinth," (I Corinthians 1:2). Unless one is willing to say that all believers were in Corinth at the time Paul wrote his first epistle to the Corinthians, he must conclude that the reference here is to a local church in Corinth. (L)

34. "Timotheus ... shall bring you into remembrance of my ways which be in Christ, as I teach every where in every church (assembly)," (I Corinthians 4:17). The fact that Paul taught in "every church" indicates that there was more than "one" church. (L)

35. "Set them to judge who are least esteemed

in the church (assembly)," (I Corinthians 6:4). Paul is giving instructions to the Corinthian church concerning their behaviour in a particular situation. Therefore, the reference is to the church at Corinth. (L)

36. "And so ordain I in all churches (assemblies)," (I Corinthians 7:17). Again, the plural usage indicates more than one church. Therefore, the reference is to local churches. (L)

37. "Give none offence, ... to the church (assembly) of God," (I Corinthians 10:32). Some argue that this refers to the totality of all believers in every place. Others feel that since Paul is writing to the church in Corinth, that only the Corinthian church is meant. (Q)

38. "We have no such custom, neither the churches (assemblies) of God," (I Corinthians 11:16). The plurality of churches mentioned here could refer to nothing but local churches. (L)

39. "When ye come together in the church (assembly), I hear that there be divisions among you," (I Corinthians 11:18). There is no question but what Paul is writing to the Corinthian church. The reference therefore, is to a local church. (L)

40. "Despise ye the church (assembly) of God?" (I Corinthians 11:22). The reference is again to the action of the Corinthian believers. (L)

41. "And God hath set some in the church (assembly), first apostles," (I Corinthians 12:28). While some feel that this must refer to the universal body of Christ, others declare rather strongly that the local church is in view here, and that God gives

these gifts to various men in every local church. (Q)

42. "He that prophesieth edifieth the church (assembly)," (I Corinthians 14:4). The context reveals that the Corinthian church is in question here. Therefore, the local church is the intended meaning. (L)

43. "Greater is he that prophesieth than he that speaketh with tongues, except he interpret, that the church (assembly) may receive edifying," (I Corinthians 14:5). One person could not speak to the universal body, nor could the universal body be edified or built up by one person speaking. Therefore, the local church at Corinth is in view here again. (L)

44. "Seek that ye may excell to the edifying of the church (assembly)." (I Corinthians 14:12). Since Paul is addressing himself to the problem in the church at Corinth, it is evident that he has reference to that particular church in this case. (L)

45. "In the church (assembly) I had rather speak five words with my understanding," (I Corinthians 14:19). Paul could not speak with understanding to the universal church, but he could to any given congregation. (L)

46. "If therefore the whole church (assembly) be come together into one place, and all speak with tongues, and there come in those that are unlearned, or unbelievers, will they not say that ye are mad?" (I Corinthians 14:23). Since it is not possible for the universal body to gather in one place on earth, it follows that the local church at Corinth is meant here. (L)

47. "If there be no interpreter, let him keep silence in the church (assembly)," (I

Corinthians 14:28). A brief glance at this Scripture portion leaves no doubt but what the local church is meant. (L)

48. "For God is not the author of confusion, but of peace, as in all churches (assemblies) of the saints," (I Corinthians 14:33). Since the plural is used, we know that local churches are meant. (L)

49. "Let your women keep silence in the churches (assemblies)," (I Corinthians 14:34). The expression "the churches" could not mean "the church." Therefore, local churches are meant. (L)

50. "It is a shame for women to speak in the church (assembly)," (I Corinthians 14:35). Since a woman could not speak in a universal assembly, it is evident that she is not to speak in a local assembly. (L)

51. "I persecuted the church (assembly) of God," (I Corinthians 15:9). (See number eight). Some feel that this refers to the total universal body, or at least to more than one local church, although the singular is used. However, it is well argued that a single local church is meant because Paul persecuted only the church in Jerusalem before his conversion. It is true that he was on his way to persecute the church in Damascus, but he was saved before he got there. Therefore, "the church" could refer to the one local church in Jerusalem. However, for argument's sake we will give benefit of the doubt and say that its usage here is questionable. (Q)

52,53. "The churches (assemblies) of Asia salute you. Aquila and Priscilla salute you much in the Lord, with the church (assembly) that is in their house," (I Corinthians 16:19). Note that there is more than one church in Asia, but only one church in Aquila and Priscilla's house. (L)

54. "Paul ... unto the church (assembly) of God which is at (in) Corinth," (II Corinthians 1:1). There should be no question but what the local church in Corinth is meant. (L)

55. "The grace of God bestowed on the churches (assemblies) of Macedonia," (II Corinthians 8:1). The plural is again used, and therefore local churches are meant. (L)

56. "We have sent with him the brother, whose praise is in the gospel throughout all the churches (assemblies)," (II Corinthians 8:18). It should be without question that local churches are meant. (L)

57. He "was also chosen of the churches (assemblies) to travel with us," (II Corinthians 8:19). That local churches are meant cannot be reasonably questioned. (L)

58. "They are the messengers of the churches (assemblies), and the glory of Christ," (II Corinthians 8:23). The plural certainly indicates more than one local church. (L)

59. "Wherefore shew ye to them, and before the churches (assemblies), the proof of your love," (II Corinthians 8:24). The churches spoken of are the local churches the messengers represent. (L)

60. "I robbed other churches (assemblies), taking wages of them, to do you service," (II Corinthians 11:8). Paul is stating that he took material support from other churches while serving the church at Corinth. (L)

61. "That which cometh upon me daily, the care of all the churches (assemblies)," (II

Corinthians 11:28). Had Paul meant the universal church, he would have said "of all the church" instead of "of all the churches." (L)

62. "Ye were inferior to other churches (assemblies)," (II Corinthians 12:13). Speaking to the Corinthian church, Paul speaks of "other churches." (L)

63. "And all the brethren which are with me, unto the churches (assemblies) of Galatia," (Galatians 1:2). Galatia had more than one church to which Paul was writing. Therefore, the word "churches" indicates various local assemblies in Galatia. (L)

64. "I persecuted the church (assembly) of God," (Galatians 1:13). See explanation under numbers eight and fifty-one. (Q)

65. "And was unknown by face unto the churches (assemblies) of Judaea which were in Christ," (Galatians 1:22). Surely, the plural indicates that there were several local churches in Judaea. (L)

66. "And hath put all things under his feet, and gave him to be the head over all things to the church (assembly), Which is his body," (Ephesians 1:22-23). By most people it is accepted without question that we find here a reference to the universal church or body of which Christ is head. Many argue that local churches could not be meant here because Christ could not be the head of many bodies. However, Paul said to the church in Corinth, "Now ye are the (a) body of Christ and members in particular," (I Corinthians 12:27). Now, if the church in Corinth was a body of Christ, then each local church must be a body of Christ. Furthermore, Paul stated, "I would

have you know, that the head of every man is Christ," (I Corinthians 11:3). If Christ could be the "head" of every man, why could He not be the "head" of every local church? While it seems more reasonable and more consistent with the rest of the Bible to think of this in terms of a local church, for the sake of argument we will call it a doubtful passage in meaning. (Q)

67. "To the intent that now unto the principalities and powers in heavenly places might be known by the church (assembly) the manifold wisdom of God," (Ephesians 3:10). This is the first usage of the word on which a strong argument for the universal church can be based. (U)

68. "Unto him be glory in the church (assembly) by Christ Jesus throughout all ages," (Ephesians 3:21). While this is another strong argument for the universal invisible church, it must be noted that the reference is to the future. (U)

69. "For the husband is the head of the wife, even as Christ is the head of the church (assembly)," (Ephesians 5:23). Many feel that this could only refer to the universal body. However, the local church could be in view here, (see argument under number sixty-six). (Q)

70. "Therefore as the church (assembly) is subject unto Christ, so let the wives be to their own husbands in every thing," (Ephesians 5:24). See the statements under numbers sixty-six and sixty-nine. (Q)

71. "Husbands, love your wives, even as Christ also loved the church (assembly), and gave himself for it," (Ephesians 5:25). See the statements under numbers

sixty-six and sixty-nine. (Q)

72. "That he might present it to himself a glorious church (assembly)," (Ephesians 5:27). While this does seem to be a reference to the totality of all believers, it must be noted that it also refers to a future date. All believers will not be assembled together until the rapture. (See also number sixty-six). (Q)

73. "For no man ever yet hated his own flesh; but nourisheth and cherisheth it, even as the Lord the church (assembly)," (Ephesians 5:29). In this verse we are told that the Lord cares for the church as a man cares for his body. This is true of the Lord in His relationship to the local churches or to the believers as a whole. (See also number sixty-six). (Q)

74. "This is a great mystery: but I speak concerning Christ and the church (assembly)," (Ephesians 5:32). There are some who dogmatically declare that this could make reference to nothing but the universal church. However, Paul said to the church in Corinth, "For I am jealous over you with godly jealousy: for I have espoused you to one husband, that I may present you as a chaste virgin to Christ," (II Corinthians 11:2). Therefore, if the Corinthian church is spoken of as the bride of Christ, why would this portion have to refer to a universal body? (Q)

75. "Concerning zeal, persecuting the church (assembly)," (Philippians 3:6). See numbers eight, fifty-one, and sixty-four. (Q)

76. "No church (assembly) communicated with me as concerning giving and receiving, but ye only," (Philippians

149

4:15). Here we see the Philippian church contrasted with other churches because the Philippian church provided for Paul's needs as he ministered, but the others did not. It is evident, then, that the local church is the intended meaning. (L)

77. "And he is the head of the body, the church (assembly)," (Colossians 1:18). See numbers sixty-six and seventy-four. (Q)

78. "The afflictions of Christ in my flesh for his body's sake, which is the church (assembly)," (Colossians 1:24). See numbers sixty-six and seventy-four. (Q)

79. "Salute the brethren which are in Laodicea, and Nymphas, and the church (assembly) which is in his house," (Colossians 4:15). The universal church could not meet in the house of Nymphas, but a local congregation could and did. (L)

80. "And when this epistle is read among you, cause that it be read also in the church (assembly) of the Laodiceans," (Colossians 4:16). No reasonable question can be brought up against the meaning of a local church in this passage. (L)

81. "Paul, and Silvanus, and Timotheus, unto the church (assembly) of the Thessalonians," (I Thessalonians 1:1). Beyond doubt this is a reference to a local church in Thessalonica. (L)

82. "For ye, brethren, became followers of the churches (assemblies) of God which in Judaea are in Christ Jesus," (I Thessalonians 2:14). The reference is to many local churches in Judaea. (L)

83. "Paul, and Silvanus, and Timotheus, unto the church (assembly) of the Thessalonians," (II Thessalonians 1:1). The church in the locality of Thessalonica

is in view. (L)

84. "We ourselves glory in you in the churches (assemblies) of God," (II Thessalonians 1:4). Since God has "churches", they must be local churches. (L)

85. "For if a man know not how to rule his own house, how shall he take care of the church (assembly) of God?" (I Timothy 3:5). Paul is clearly speaking of one man being the pastor of one local church. (L)

86. "That thou mayest know how thou (one) oughtest to behave thyself in the (a) house of God, which is the church (a church) (an assembly) of the living God, the pillar and ground of the truth," (I Timothy 3:15). This passage obviously teaches that an assembly is a house of God. Here, the assembly spoken of is the one in Ephesus. Therefore, each local assembly is a house of God. (L)

87. "If any man or woman that believeth have widows, let them relieve them, and let not the church (assembly) be charged; that it may relieve them that are widows indeed," (I Timothy 5:16). Only a local assembly would be able to follow these instructions. (L)

88. "And to our beloved Apphia, and Archippus our fellowsoldier, and to the church (assembly) in thy house," (Philemon 2). The church in Philemon's house would of necessity be a local church. (L)

89. "In the midst of the church (assembly) will I sing praise unto thee," (Hebrews 2:12). This quote from the Old Testament was originally made in reference to Israel, but here is used in reference to the church. Since Israel was a congregation of people, this may also refer to a congregation. (Q)

151

90. "The general assembly and church (assembly) of the firstborn, which are written in heaven," (Hebrews 12:23). This is a strong argument for the universal position. However, it must be noted that positional truth is being dealt with instead of present reality. (Q)

91. "Is any sick among you? let him call for the elders of the church (assembly)," (James 5:14). The elders to be called for must be from a local church. (L)

92. "Which have borne witness of thy charity before the church (assembly)," (III John 6). One could not bear a witness before the universal church, but could before a local church. (L)

93. "I wrote unto the church (assembly)," (III John 9). Paul had written to the local church of which Gaius was a part. (L)

94. Diotrephes "casteth them out of the church (assembly)," (III John 10). Diotrephes could not remove anyone from the body of Christ, but could and did remove various ones from a local church. (L)

95. "John to the seven churches (assemblies) which are in Asia," (Revelation 1:4). There should be no question but what local churches are meant. (L)

96. "Send it unto the seven churches (assemblies) which are in Asia," (Revelation 1:11). Since there are seven churches in Asia, the reference could not be to a single universal church. (L)

97,98. "The seven stars are the angels of the seven churches (assemblies): and the seven candlesticks which thou sawest are the seven churches (assemblies)," (Revelation 1:20). There is no question, local churches are meant. (L)

99. "Unto the angel of the church (assembly) of Ephesus," (Revelation 2:1). Ephesus is one of the seven local churches. (L)

100. "He that hath an ear, let him hear what the Spirit saith unto the churches (assemblies)," (Revelation 2:7). The plurality of churches indicates local churches. (L)

101. "Unto the angel of the church (assembly) in Smyrna," (Revelation 2:8). Smyrna was one of the seven local churches in Asia. (L)

102. "He that hath an ear, let him hear what the Spirit saith unto the churches (assemblies)," (Revelation 2:11). The plurality of churches indicates local churches. (L)

103. "To the angel of the church (assembly) in Pergamos," (Revelation 2:12). Pergamos was one of the seven local churches in Asia. (L)

104. "He that hath an ear, let him hear what the Spirit saith unto the churches (assemblies)," (Revelation 2:17). The plurality of churches indicates local churches. (L)

105. "Unto the angel of the church (assembly) in Thyatira," (Revelation 2:18). Thyatira was one of the seven local churches in Asia. (L)

106. "All the churches (assemblies) shall know that I am he," (Revelation 2:23). Christ is speaking of "all churches", therefore, local churches are meant. (L)

107. "He that hath an ear, let him hear what the Spirit saith unto the churches (assemblies)," (Revelation 2:29). The plurality of churches indicates local churches. (L)

108. "Unto the angel of the church (assembly) in Sardis," (Revelation 3:1). Sardis was one of the seven local churches in Asia. (L)

109. "He that hath an ear, let him hear what the

Spirit saith unto the churches (assemblies)," (Revelation 3:6). The plurality of churches indicates local churches. (L)

110. "To the angel of the church (assembly) in Philadelphia," (Revelation 3:7). Philadelphia was one of the seven local churches in Asia. (L)

111. "Unto the angel of the church (assembly) of the Laodiceans," (Revelation 3:14). Since the word "church" is used in reference to seven different churches in seven different localities in Asia, it is obvious that local churches are meant. (L)

112. "I Jesus have sent mine angel to testify unto you these things in the churches (assemblies)," (Revelation 22:16). This last usage of the word clearly and unmistakably refers to local churches. (L)

After examining all one hundred and twelve times that the word appears in the New Testament, and being as liberal as possible toward the universal church concept, it is a fact beyond reasonable doubt that the New Testament usage of the word church, ekklasia, is used almost exclusively to refer to a particular local assembly. Without any doubt, the word refers to a local church or to local churches ninety-one times, which is eighty-one percent of the total. Giving as much benefit as possible to the universal theory, only nineteen of the passages are left with uncertainty, doubt, or question, which is only about seventeen percent of the total. However, each of these have a very reasonable and logical explanation in favor of the local church concept and, therefore, should be accepted to refer to a local church since the word is used in that sense without doubt eighty-one percent of the time. To fail to follow that hermeneutical principle would be like teaching that one must be baptized in order to be saved because there are a few difficult passages which seem to imply that. We must be consistent in our method of interpreting the Bible. If we accept these passages as references to local churches, then the word is used in the New Testament in that sense over ninety-eight percent of the time. It is also interesting to note that there are only two passages which give evidence of a universal invisible church which is the single body or bride of Christ. It must not be overlooked, however, that these passages view the church in prospect. There will be no universal church (assembly) of all believers until the rapture. At that time in the future, all believers will be assembled together in one great assembly (church) at one time. In studying this or any other subject of Scripture, we must always keep one basic principle of interpretation before us. We must interpret every word by its usual literal meaning unless the facts of the context or other related passages clearly indicate that we should understand it otherwise. Following this principle, it seems best to understand all references to a "church" as a reference to a local assembly. This can be done even with the two passages which seem to refer to a universal church, because the immediate context allows it, and it is in accord with other clear passages of Scripture.

THE DEVELOPMENT OF CHURCH

FROM SCRIPTURE

We have seen that the New Testament emphasis upon the word "ekklasia" is that of an individual local assembly. It should also be noted that the Old Testament word for congregation, "kahal", is translated with the Greek word "ekklasia" in the Septuagint. Kahal means "congregation", and is used in reference to the congregation of Israel in the wilderness. Therefore, when Christ or the apostles used the word ekklasia, the Jews understood it to mean a congregation or assembly of people under the direction of God. The Greeks used the word to refer to a regularly called assembly in which the citizens of a free state came together to discuss and make decisions on matters of public business. Therefore, when Christ and the apostles used the word "ekklasia", the Greeks understood it to mean an assembly which had been called together for democratic action. Its usage in Scripture, then, is always to emphasize the assembly more than the calling out. In all English versions of the New Testament before the translation of the King James Version, the word "ekklasia" was translated with the word "congregation" or "assembly." The only reason that it was translated as "church" in the King James Version is because King James gave an order to the translators not to translate the word as assembly or congregation. Therefore, we have much confusion surrounding the concept of the church that will most likely never be clarified in most minds.

FROM HISTORY

Since the word "church" is clearly used in reference to a local church or assembly, how; then, has there come to be such an overwhelming emphasis upon the universal invisible church concept in this generation? The answer is to be found in church history. In the third century, the church of Rome advocated a universal visible church theory, hence, the Roman Catholic (universal) church. This concept grew, and by the sixteenth century was embedded deeply in the theological thinking of almost all who professed christianity. In the sixteenth century, the Protestant Reformation took place and many found themselves withdrawing from the universal (Catholic) visible church. This they could not do with good conscience, so they began to place more emphasis upon the universal invisible spiritual church so as to justify their actions of coming out of the visible Catholic (universal) church. As the years passed, the concept was more widely accepted among Protestants, and the King James Version of the Bible came on the scene using the word "church" instead of "assembly." Some forty years ago the concept got another boost during the fundamentalist-modernist debate. Many believers who did not understand the battle which was taking place withdrew from local churches because they did not think that the arguing and fighting was right, and began to embrace what they thought was the "true" church where there were no differences. This concept has grown rapidly since that time, has become the mother of the present ecumenical movement, and has fostered the present prevalent feeling that local church membership is not important because membership in the "true universal invisible church" which is the "body of Christ" is all that is necessary.

In conclusion it must be noted that when one begins to emphasize the universal body over the local body, he also begins to get away from personal responsibility to the church and the Lord. Let us forever keep the emphasis where the Lord placed it in His Word!

BIBLIOGRAPHY

Bancroft, Emery H., *Elemental Theology*, Grand Rapids, Zondervan Publishing House, 1963.

Berkhof, L., *Systematic Theology*, Grand Rapids, Wm. B. Eerdmans Publishing Company, 1965.

Bernard, J.H., *Cambridge Greek New Testament for Schools and Colleges — The Pastoral Epistles*, Cambridge, The University Press, 1906.

Berry, George Ricker, *The Interlinear Greek-English New Testament*, Grand Rapids, Zondervan Publishing House, 1969.

Conybeare, W.J., and Howson, J.S., *The Life and Epistles of St. Paul*, Grand Rapids, Wm. B. Eerdmans Publishing Company, 1959.

Cooper, David L., *The World's Greatest Library Graphically Illustrated*, Los Angeles, Biblical Research Society, 1961.

Cooper, David L., *What Men Must Believe*, Los Angeles, Biblical Research Society, 1953.

Emmaus Bible School, Staff, *What Christians Believe*, Chicago, Moody Press, 1951.

Evans, William, *The Great Doctrines of the Bible*, Chicago, Moody Press, 1949.

Fuller, David Otis, *Which Bible?*, Grand Rapids, International Publications, 1971.

Green, Thomas Sheldon, *A Greek-English Lexicon of the New Testament*, Grand Rapids, Zondervan Publishing House, 1971.

Hodge, Charles, *Systematic Theology*, Grand Rapids, Wm. B. Eerdmans Publishing Company, 1970.

Ironside, H.A., *Lectures on the Epistle to the Romans*, New Jersey, Loizeaux Brothers, Inc., 1970.

Murray, Andrew, *The Ministry of Intercession*, New Jersey, Fleming H. Revell Company, 1964.

Newell, William R., *Romans Verse by Verse*, Chicago, Moody Press, 1938.

Nicoll, W. Robertson, Editor, *The Expositors Greek Testament*, Grand Rapids, Wm. B. Eerdmans Publishing Company, 1970.

Orr, James, General Editor, *The International Standard Bible Encyclopedia*, Vol. I, Grand Rapids, Wm. B. Eerdmans Publishing Company, 1939.

Ray, Jasper James, *God Wrote Only One Bible*, Junction City, Oregon, The Eye Opener Publishers, 1955.

Rice, John R., *Prayer — Asking and Receiving*, Murfreesboro, Tennessee, Sword of the Lord Publishers, 1964.

Rotherham, Joseph Bryant, *The Emphasized Bible*, Grand Rapids, Kregel Publications, 1971.

Shedd, William G.T., *Dogmatic Theology*, Grand Rapids, Zondervan Publishing House, 1971.

Strauss, Lehman, *The Book of the Revelation*, New Jersey, Loizeaux Brothers, Inc., 1967.

Strong, Augustus H., *Systematic Theology*, Philadelphia, The Judson Press, 1960.

Strong, James, *The Exhaustive Concordance of the Bible*, New York, Abingdon Press, 1958.

Telford, Andrew, *Subjects of Sovereignty*, Boca Raton, Florida, Published by author, n.d.

The Analytical Greek Lexicon, New York, Harper and Brothers Publishers, n.d.

Torrey, R. A., *How to Work For Christ*, New Jersey, Fleming H. Revell Company, n.d.

Vincent, Marvin R., *Word Studies in the New Testament*, Grand Rapids, Wm. B. Eerdmans Publishing Company, 1969.

Vine, W.E., *An Expository Dictionary of New Testament Words*, Westwood, N.J., Fleming H. Revell Company, 1966.

Wuest, Kenneth S., *Word Studies in the Greek New Testament*, Grand Rapids, Wm. B. Eerdmans Publishing Company, 1973.